The Complete Book of **BASIC BRUSHSTROKES** *for* **DECORATIVE PAINTERS**

The Complete Book of
BASIC BRUSHSTROKES
for DECORATIVE PAINTERS

SHARON STANSIFER CDA

NORTH LIGHT BOOKS
CINCINNATI, OHIO
www.nlbooks.com

About the Author

Sharon Stansifer CDA, a lifelong artist, has been teaching decorative painting classes throughout the country since 1991. She has designed and published many project packets and has had articles published in decorative painting magazines. Sharon has won several top awards for her artwork and also paints private commissions. She is currently teaching painting classes in Mission Viejo, California. In 1999, Sharon received the Master Decorative Artist (MDA) certification in Strokework. She resides in Trabuco Canyon, California, with her husband and two sons.

Other fine North Light Books are available from your local bookstore, art supply store or direct from the publisher.

03 02 01 00   5 4 3 2

Library of Congress Cataloging-in-Publication Data

Stansifer, Sharon.
   The complete book of basic brushtrokes for decorative painters / Sharon Stansifer.
     p.   cm.
  Includes index.
  ISBN 0-89134-922-7 (alk. paper)
  1. Painting—Technique. 2. Brushwork. 3. Decoration and ornament. I. Title
TT385.S73   1999
745.7'23—dc21   99-14770
                                               CIP

Editor: Roseann Biederman
Production Editor: Christine Doyle
Production Coordinator: Erin Boggs
Designer: Brian Roeth
Photographer: Christine Polomsky

Dedication

This book is dedicated to my family: my wonderful, supportive husband, Laurence (Laurie), and my two sons, Ryan and Kyle. Thank you for being so understanding all those many times I was too busy painting or writing this book.

Laurie—Through good and bad you always seem to support my love for painting and teaching. May the love and support you give me always be returned and multiplied to you.

Ryan—I could not have done this book without you! You have been my right hand with all the computer work you have done. You have become amazingly good at interpreting my handwritten scribbles. You are always there to jump on the computer no matter the quantity of work and short deadline. I hope all the work you have done on this book will speed you in conquering your future businesses. Heaven help me when you leave home!

Kyle—You are such a joy in my life and have really made a huge difference with all your help the last year writing this book. I have the feeling I'm seeing the beginning of a wonderful chef! It has been so much help to have your creativity at work, in the kitchen and out. Your eye for color and your hints and observations on my paintings have come to my aid many times. Thank you for always being so encouraging and supportive.

To my parents, Keith and Sara, thank you for always encouraging me to be my best and work hard. May I always make you feel proud and feel loved.

To my sister, Brenda, may you be as blessed as I have been, make and teach teddy bear designs, and let your creativity (which is considerable) and talent flow and grow.

A supportive and committed family can make the difference of being able to take on a huge project like this. Thank you my loving family for making it possible for me to fulfill this dream.

Acknowledgments

This is the hardest part of the book to write. When I think of who has been helpful and inspiring to me in writing this book, so many people come to mind. I have had so much love, support and encouragement from my family, friends, teachers and students.

Thank you so much to my students (especially my ongoing students). You have been the driving force in keeping me working so hard at continually improving my teaching skills. Working with all of you has been such a blessing; you make hard work fun and rewarding. I know I have succeeded if I make a difference in your lives!

Special thanks to my dear friend Yuko Culliney, CDA, who taught me, "When you don't keep learning, your students will catch up with you." (I've been working hard ever since!) You have been so inspiring and supportive and such a wonderful friend! May we always stay close friends—painting or otherwise.

To my good friend JoAnn Seel, thank you for all your many prayers, encouagement and love. You are the kind of friend everyone wants but few (like me) are blessed with. I love you!

Special thanks to my friend Janet Cattolica for your help with prepping all the projects in this book and your proofreading expertise. You were the difference between missing and making many deadlines.

Thank you Barbara Carson with Delta Technical Coatings for always quickly providing your beautiful paints for my design needs.

Thank you Daler-Rowney for supplying Robert Simmons Expressions Brushes. I love these brushes!

And last but not least, thank you David Lewis, Greg Albert, Kathy Kipp and Roseann Biederman for making this book possible. I appreciate your faith in me and all of your support.

TABLE OF CONTENTS

DAISY STRIPED BOX

RUNNING ROSES WALL SCONCE

POINSETTIA TRAY

PANSY FAN BOX

HYDRANGEA AND ROSES SEWING BOX

INTRODUCTION

Decorative art is an amazing world. It spans from primitive folk art to incredibly realistic painting with the look of fine art. It encompasses such a wide range of designs that I always find it difficult to answer the question, "What kind of art do you do?"

The decorative art field has amazing variation. Look around your house—at your sofa, wallpaper, bedspreads, the salt and pepper shakers in your kitchen and your other furniture pieces. Such beauty surrounds us, and it all falls into the decorative art field. Decorative artists also paint those beautiful paintings on your walls! Our inspiration comes from opening our eyes to everything around us and painting what we find on useful and beautiful items for our homes and offices.

One big difference between decorative art and fine art is the learning method. Decorative art is taught in a step-by-step style of teaching. Students learning in this art field do not draw their own designs. Instead they learn basic techniques with a previously designed drawing and then continually learn new techniques to add to what they learned before. In learning this way, everyone can learn to paint! So many people have come to me seeing themselves as having "no talent"—they are now painting beautifully with this method of learning.

In designing this book, my goal has been to reflect this style of teaching to the degree that no one will feel he or she does not have the talent to do

these paintings. By breaking down steps into even smaller steps, anyone can learn basic strokes, which is the perfect place to begin and build from.

Learning brushstroke techniques can be the best tool to build with, for the beginner, intermediate or advanced painter. I first started with stroke work to learn strokes, but I found it gave me an unexpected and much needed benefit: *brush control*.

By learning the techniques in this book, you will be able to make the brush do what you want it to do. I have found that all aspects of painting are improved, no matter what style of painting you wish to eventually paint.

Each stroke in this book is broken down into several steps. Practicing will be the key to achieving control with these strokes and will help you make your strokes look consistent. In your first few practice sheets, you may find only one or two strokes that have the desired shape, but with continued practice, you will find your strokes becoming more and more consistent.

I have included Directional Angle Sheets to help you visualize and make your practicing more effective. I have found students who use these sheets learn the strokes more rapidly and gain control over their various brushes.

The finished projects in this book will allow you to put the basic skills you have learned into practice. They are simple (graduating to a little more difficult) yet beautiful functional pieces for your home.

May your future be filled with beautiful paintings.

Sharon Stansifer, CDA

CHAPTER 1

Brushes

Over the last several years, I have used many types and brands of brushes. Selecting your brushes can be a confusing and overwhelming process (like walking into the cosmetic department of your favorite large department store).

There is no way I can stress the importance of working with good quality brushes. I have seen so many painters struggle to create beautiful work using cheaper brushes. Don't make things more difficult on yourself! Your biggest and best investment in all of decorative painting is your brushes. You don't want to spend lots of time trying to create beautiful strokes only to find what has made them not look right is simply a lousy brush.

The brushes I currently work with are called Robert Simmons Expressions by Daler-Rowney. I prefer these to other brushes for a few reasons. First, I have found they have high-quality bristles that perform well. Second, they have a larger (in diameter) handle. In 1996, after having three years of severe problems and pain with my right wrist (of course, the one I paint with), the doctors found it had been broken for those three years! I went through surgery to pin and wire it back together. While it is better than it was, I still have a lot of difficulty and limitations.

One of the things my doctors and physical therapists said was that I had to work with a larger grip (or handle). The smaller the grip, the more stress my hand and wrist would be under, creating fatigue and pain.

I was thrilled when Robert Simmons came out with these larger grip

These are the brushes I used to paint the strokes and projects in this book. They include flats, rounds, angle shaders, filberts and script liners.

handles. After using them, I found I could paint longer before I had the fatigue and pain that interfered with the thing I loved to do the most: painting.

I have worked with so many people who have hand and wrist difficulties. These brushes are a way to alleviate symptoms as well as to avoid developing future problems.

Make sure when purchasing your brushes for projects in this book that they have Golden Taklon bristles and that they are artist quality (not crafter quality). This will help you make more

beautiful strokes and will make the painting process more enjoyable.

In this book we will be using flats, filberts, rounds, angle shaders and script liners. This will help you learn to use the various brush shapes and loading techniques. I have specified certain sizes of these differently shaped brushes, but it is best to experiment with several sizes in each shape. Also practice different loading techniques with all the various shapes and sizes of brushes.

CHAPTER 2

Basic Supplies

Paints

The paints used in this book are Delta bottled acrylics. When choosing paints to practice and paint your stroke work, look for good paint consistency. If your paint is very thick, add a touch of water to slightly thin the paint. I have found Delta paints to be excellent in paint consistency, and they have good coverage and the widest range of colors.

Any good quality bottled acrylic paints may be used for the strokework and the projects in this book. I like Delta Ceramcoat's paint consistency and wide array of colors.

Transfer Paper

Transfer paper is thin sheets of paper coated on one side with black, gray or white graphite (also available in yellow and red). This is very different than carbon paper. Carbon paper has *ink* on one side where transfer paper has graphite (the difference between a pen and a pencil). Never use carbon paper; the ink will smear and make a mess.

When transferring the pattern to the painting surface, trace over the pattern as lightly as possible with a stylus (or a pencil). If you press too hard, the transfer lines will be too dark and hard to cover, and you will dent the wood. Your goal is to transfer lines as lightly as possible and still be able to see them.

The photos at right and at the top of the next page show how to transfer your pattern onto your basecoated surface.

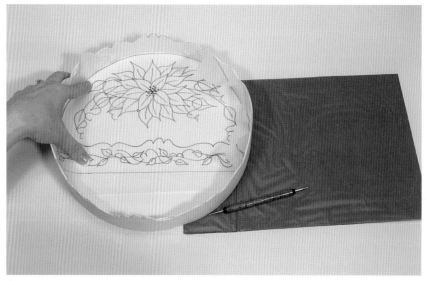

Once you carefully traced your pattern onto tracing or tissue paper, place it on your basecoated piece and secure it with a few pieces of tape.

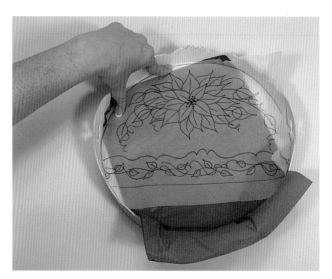

Since my tray is basecoated in a light color, I'm using a dark color of transfer paper such as black or gray to make my lines show up more easily.

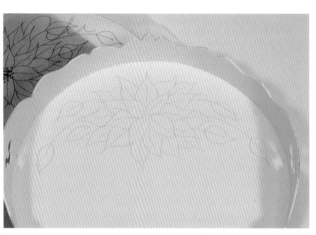

With the graphite transfer paper under the pattern, I trace over the lines with a stylus, using very little pressure to avoid denting the wood underneath.

Try to transfer your pattern as neatly and precisely as you can. Poorly traced lines can cause confusion once you begin painting.

Transferring the border pattern onto the outside edge of the tray will make it easier to keep the design neat and straight.

Dry-It-Board

This handy little tool will speed your preparation time on your painting. When sealing or basecoating your wood pieces, simply apply the sealer (or base coat) to one side of the surface, lay the wet side down on the Dry-It-Board and continue to seal (or basecoat) the other surfaces. The board will allow air circulation over all the surfaces at one time.

Tack Cloth

Tack cloth is a cheesecloth covered with wax. Open the cloth and very lightly dust over the surface after sanding or using steel wool. The purpose of this step is to remove any remaining wood or steel "dust." Use the tack cloth as if you were dusting, not polishing, furniture.

Sanding Pads

Each color of 3M's sanding pads has two different sanding strengths. Use the red pad for the rougher pieces of wood and the yellow for the smoother wood pieces that need less work. (If you cannot find these pads, substitute #240, 320, 400 and 600 wet/dry sandpaper.)

Foam Brushes

Foam brushes are perfect for applying wood sealer to raw wood pieces. They come in several sizes. Choose the width of the brush according to the size of your painting surface.

Brush Basin

A brush basin is a great little water container that will save wear and tear on your brushes. Fill both sides of the basin with cool water about one-half inch below the center divider. Rubbing your brush (at the metal ferrule) over the washboard side will help massage the paint out of your brush. Also, you can rest your brush in the other side for a few minutes until you have time to wash it out.

White and Gray Chalk Pencils

Chalk pencils come in very handy and work better on painting surfaces than a regular graphite pencil. The chalk lines can be easily removed with water or an eraser.

Palette Paper

Palette paper is bound into a pad that you can tear off in sheets. When selecting a palette paper pad for acrylic paints, check that one side of each paper is waxed. This will make sure the paper does not absorb the water from your acrylic paint. You will be using your acrylic palette when blending your paints.

Wet Palette

To keep your paints from drying out too quickly, use a wet palette, a product that consists of a plastic container and sponge. Wet the sponge, squeeze out only some of the water, and lay the sponge in the bottom of the container. Place the palette paper on top of the sponge and let soak. Using this wet paper for your acrylic paints will give you more time to work with them before they dry. I use Masterson's Wet Palette.

Buy the best quality supplies you can afford. In time you will discover your own favorites. Shown here are most of the materials I used to produce the projects in this book. They're described in detail in the text.

The Complete Book of Basic Brushstrokes for Decorative Painters

Neutral Gel

This product slows down the drying time of acrylic paints, giving you more time to blend your paint before it dries. Mix the Neutral Gel with paint to create a transparent effect (stain-like) without changing the paint consistency.

Matte Spray

After your base coat is completely dry, lightly spray your surface two to three times with a matte spray, such as the one made by Delta. Applying this product will protect your background and allow easy cleanup for mistakes. After the matte spray is dry, lightly rub #0000 steel wool over all sprayed surfaces. Use your tack cloth to remove steel dust, and transfer your pattern onto your surface.

Water-Based Varnish

After your painting is finished, apply several thin coats of varnish, such as Delta Water-Based Varnish, over the entire surface to protect all your hard work. The varnishes come in matte (no shine), satin (medium shine) and gloss (glassy shine).

Stylus

I always tell my students that your stylus is "the wooden thing with metal poky ends"; not very professional, but it works visually. The stylus has two sizes for the small metal balls on the ends. These will be used for transferring patterns or making "dip-dot" designs (dip the metal end into fresh paint and dot onto your surface to form a beautiful round dot).

If acrylic paints dry too fast for you, mix in some Neutral Gel with a palette knife to gain some blending time.

Large Stylus (Embossing Tool)

Same as a stylus, with large metal balls on each end.

Eraser

Magic Rub Eraser is a great gentle eraser that will not disturb paint while erasing graphite lines.

Metal Primer

Delta Metal Primer is a wonderful product that is evenly painted onto the clean tin surface with a brush. After the primer is completely dry, feel the surface with your fingers; if needed, lightly sand with your yellow sanding pad (or #400-#600 wet/dry sandpaper), then basecoat with paint as usual.

Brush Cleaner

The care of your brushes is critical to creating beautiful decorative painting—especially stroke work. Each time you paint, use your brush cleaner to remove all the paint from your brushes. You will be amazed at how much longer your brushes will last. Reshape your clean brushes to their original shape, and allow to dry.

Wood Sealer

I prefer a water-based sealer to an oil-based product. It dries quickly and doesn't upset my allergies. Your wood will be much smoother by using the sealer (and sanding). After you basecoat, it will be much easier to paint on and nicer to the touch. Taking time to properly prepare your surface will really show in the finished product.

Steel Wool (#0000)

Generally purchased at any hardware store, steel wool is used to slightly buff a surface after varnishing or matte spraying. This will allow paint to grab to the surface after basecoating. When needed, between finished layers of varnish, steel wool will polish a surface for a glasslike, smooth texture.

Palette Knife

These handy little tools come in plastic and metal. The plastic palette knife is inexpensive and a good way to start; metal palette knives are much stronger and last a long time. Use your palette knife to mix paints and transfer paint puddles (if needed) to other surfaces.

Paper Towels

Quality paper towels can make painting much easier. Shop towels (they are blue and found in automotive departments of stores) are very thick and absorbent. If you can't find those, try Viva Ultra.

Acetate Sheets

It can be very helpful to see the book practice sheets and the Directional Angle Sheets when you begin practicing your strokes. To do this, I have begun using acetate sheets as practice overlays. These are the same sheets used on overhead projectors. You can purchase them in any office supply store. As you practice your strokes, you can clean them off and use them again or just throw them away and use another one. Once you feel more comfortable with the strokes, switch to bristol board or posterboard.

Bristol Board (or Posterboard)

These work great for practice sheets. Basecoat the bristol board with a medium-color paint (I like Lavender Lace; it's easy on the eyes and most any color shows well for practicing). Purchase sheets that are 8½″ × 11″ (21cm × 28cm) or cut a larger piece into this size after the base coat is dry. Keep several sheets handy so you can practice for a few minutes anytime you wish. Keep these sheets in a notebook and number and date them for future reference.

If needed, draw directional lines onto the practice boards to help you angle the chisel of the brush for pulling your strokes. The white chalk pencil works great for these lines.

CHAPTER 3

Getting Started

Setting up a comfortable work area is critical to your painting. You do not need a lot of room—the area I paint on is a small desk that fits into a wet bar area. You do need to be able to rest your forearm up to the elbow of your painting hand, and you need room for your palette, a water container and your brushes.

Remember, the more relaxed you are, the better your strokes will be. People typically tense up when getting ready to do stroke work, so it may take some concentration to avoid this. I always try to put my feet on a stool and have a small pillow to support my lower back.

It will save you time, energy and effort if you set up the supplies you need before you start. Tear off a couple of paper towels and fold them in quarters. Put clean, cold water in your brush basin and set up your small wet palette and acrylic palette, and your brushes and practice sheets.

Practice Sheets

Clear acetate and posterboard both work well as practice sheets. Since acetate sheets are transparent, you can lay them over any page in the book to practice your aim when pulling the strokes. These sheets can be wiped off and used again. The easiest way to start is by laying the transparent acetate sheets over the Directional practice sheet on pages 18 and 19. The benefit of starting with acetate sheets is that you will be able to see your guidelines through the pages so you can aim the brush in the proper direction for each individual type of stroke.

Posterboard also works well. Prepare the board ahead of time by basecoating the entire surface. Posterboard is sold in 22″×28″ (55cm× 71cm) sheets. It is easiest to paint it first (it will take about 2 ounces of paint to basecoat the entire sheet) then cut it into six pieces, each

8½″×11″ (21cm×28cm). These pieces will be easy to handle and fit neatly into a notebook or folder for reference. Basecoating is necessary to seal the surface, so it will not absorb water from your brush while you practice your stroke. If you practice on posterboard or paper that is not basecoated, you may be misled about the paint consistency required for the actual project.

When basecoating your posterboard, choose a medium, preferably neutral color, e.g., soft gray or blue. By using a medium color, both light and dark practice strokes will be easy to see. Use colors you like to look at so practicing will be more enjoyable.

Paint Palette

It is important to keep your paints workable while you paint. If you simply squeeze your paints onto a regular acrylic palette, your paints will start getting tacky. The weather has a big effect on how long acrylic paints will stay workable. The best painting temperature is about 68 degrees with moisture in the air. If it is hotter or drier, the moisture in your paint will evaporate more quickly, making it difficult to maintain a proper consistency.

A wet palette will help keep your paints workable and save you a lot of paint. These are available in small, medium and large sizes—choose the one you need by how many paint colors you will be working with. The small one works great most of the time and doesn't take up a lot of room in your painting area. The wet palette comes in handy if you are interrupted a lot during your painting like I am. Simply snap the lid on and your paints will stay fresh for days. You can also make a temporary wet palette by folding several paper towels together and dipping them in water. Wring out some (not all) of the water, then lay the wet paper towels onto your acrylic palette and smooth out. Cover the wet towels with a thin deli-style paper to allow the moisture to come through without letting the paper fall apart.

Making It Fun

There is no doubt about it: To create beautiful stroke work you must be willing to practice. The more you practice, the more control you will have over your brush and the results. But don't despair! There are ways to make stroke work practice enjoyable—even fun. As mentioned earlier, choose quiet, relaxing colors that you enjoy for your backgrounds. Stay away from bright, intense color; they tend to fatigue your eyes. Look around your home to discover the colors you like living with. If you have a favorite room, pay extra attention to the colors in it that make you feel contented—now you have your colors! When you grow tired of working with colors, find new favorites.

Another way to make practice fun is to be creative. While the strokes you make may not be perfect, you may find a lot of fun things in them. I have great fun playing with my own and my students' practice sheets to discover the shapes hidden in them—kind of like "Where's Waldo?" or "What do you see in the ink blot?" You can find leaf strokes that look like caterpillars! Turn a half leaf stroke to the side, add a couple of antennae, and you have a snail to put in your garden. Not-so-great S-strokes can be anything from a string of beans to snakes. Keep an open mind and allow yourself to have fun.

We can often be our own worst critic. When you start practicing your strokes and they don't look exactly like the ones in the book, frustration can set in. Remember, there is a beginning, middle and end to every endeavor. Those first pages of practice strokes are very important. Mark them in the order in which you paint them. They will show how you have improved with practice. Comparing those pages can be encouraging and fun.

The Complete Book of Basic Brushstrokes for Decorative Painters

Brush Control

Getting into a comfortable and natural body position makes all the difference in creating a well-shaped stroke. Every person has a natural range of motion to their arm. You will need to pay close attention to your body position and work hard to stay as relaxed as possible, especially through your arm, hand and shoulders. This may sound odd because when we think of doing something perfectly, we tend to tense up.

Because "pulling a stroke" is made as one continuous pulling motion with the brush, the motion actually comes from your shoulder. To get the feel of motion, do some pretend practice movements in the air. Without a brush in your hand, rest your entire forearm on a table or the area where you are going to paint. While remaining relaxed, start moving your entire arm clockwise, from the shoulder first, making large circles. Then make large circles with your arm counterclockwise. As you make these air strokes, concentrate on how your hand and arm feel; this way, when you are actually pulling your strokes, you can check how much tension is there. Giving counterpressure to your painting hand can really help to steady your hand. This is an isometric exercise. It's a matter of two objects with equally applied force coming from opposite directions and resulting in no movement. Get as much of your forearm rested on your painting table, with brush in hand, and have your painting hand in position to make the stroke or linework. Rest your assisting arm on the table and apply counterpressure with your assisting fingers or hand. Apply equal pressure hand to hand and notice how steady your hand is. Now you're ready!

Brush Anatomy

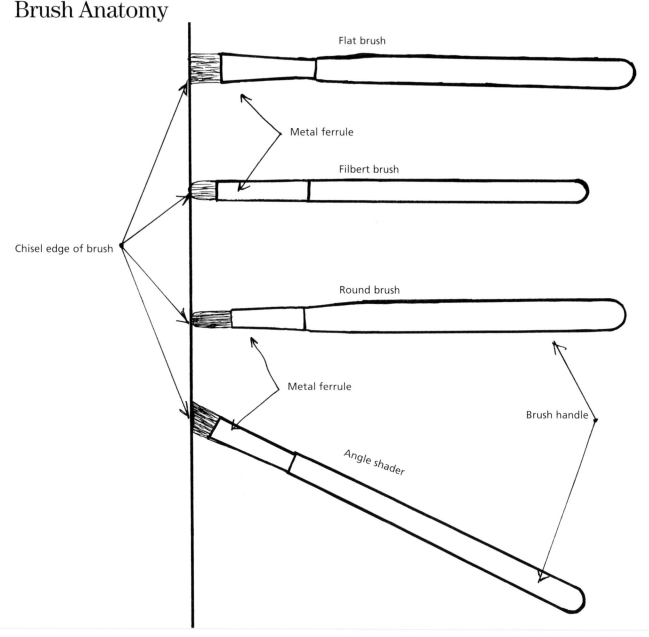

Flat brush

Metal ferrule

Filbert brush

Chisel edge of brush

Round brush

Metal ferrule

Brush handle

Angle shader

Directional Guide for the Left-Handed Painter

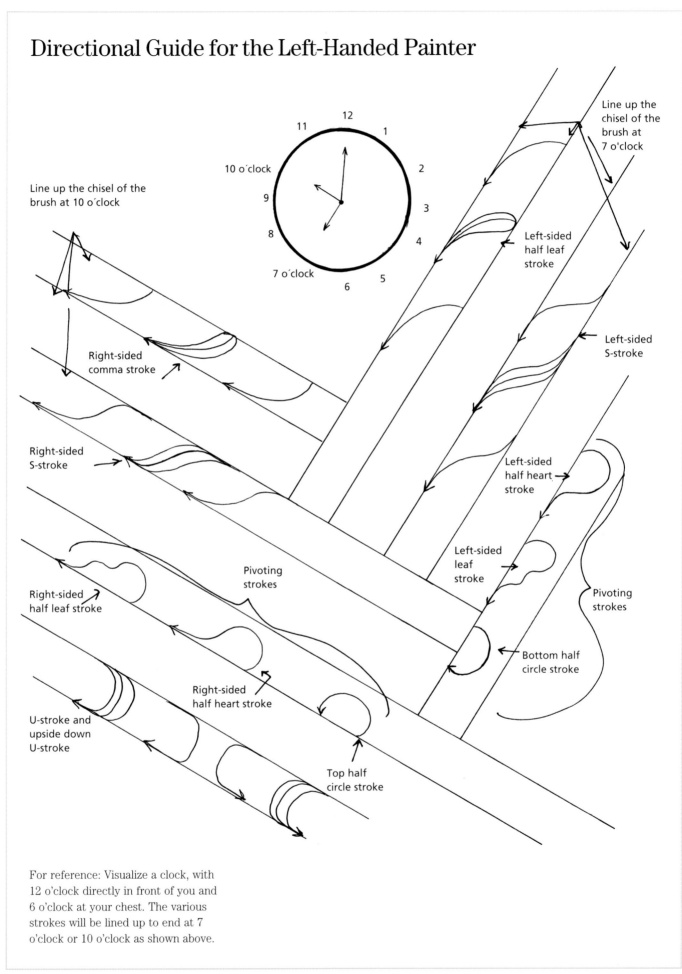

Line up the chisel of the brush at 7 o'clock

10 o´clock

7 o´clock

Line up the chisel of the brush at 10 o´clock

Left-sided half leaf stroke

Right-sided comma stroke

Left-sided S-stroke

Right-sided S-stroke

Left-sided half heart stroke

Left-sided leaf stroke

Pivoting strokes

Pivoting strokes

Right-sided half leaf stroke

Bottom half circle stroke

Right-sided half heart stroke

U-stroke and upside down U-stroke

Top half circle stroke

For reference: Visualize a clock, with 12 o'clock directly in front of you and 6 o'clock at your chest. The various strokes will be lined up to end at 7 o'clock or 10 o'clock as shown above.

Directional Guide for the Right-Handed Painter

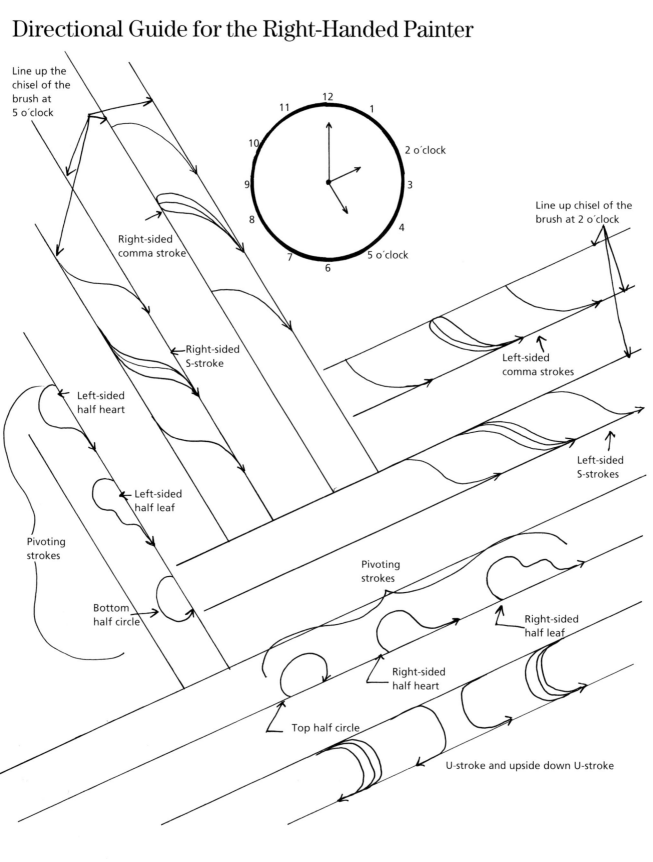

Line up the chisel of the brush at 5 o'clock

Right-sided comma stroke

Right-sided S-stroke

Left-sided half heart

Left-sided half leaf

Pivoting strokes

Bottom half circle

12
11
1
10
2 o'clock
9
3
8
4
7
6
5 o'clock

Line up chisel of the brush at 2 o'clock

Left-sided comma strokes

Left-sided S-strokes

Pivoting strokes

Right-sided half leaf

Right-sided half heart

Top half circle

U-stroke and upside down U-stroke

For reference: Visualize a clock with 12 o'clock directly in front of you and 6 o'clock at your chest. The various strokes will end at 2 o'clock or 5 o'clock.

CHAPTER 4

Single-Loaded Brush Strokes

How to Load the Brush

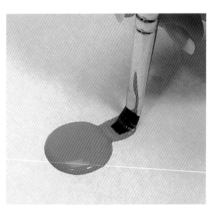

1 Pour a small puddle of fresh paint onto your wet palette. Lay a damp brush in the outer edge of the paint; applying pressure to keep brush flattened, pull a small "track" out from the puddle.

2 Flip the brush completely over and repeat on the other side of the brush (repeat these two steps as needed to fully load the brush).

Right-Sided Comma Stroke

1 Keeping the brush handle straight up-and-down from the surface of the painting, set the chisel of the brush down to begin the stroke. Make sure the chisel edge is at the same angle that the stroke will *end*.

2 Continuing to keep the brush handle straight up-and-down, put pressure on the bristles of the brush, letting the bristles lie to the side until you reach what I call the "bottom of the bounce." A synthetic brush has a natural spring to the bristles. Apply pressure slowly to the brush until you feel resistance, then stop applying pressure. Do not press beyond this point. At this point you are not actively moving the brush, you are only applying pressure.

Blending the Paint on the Brush

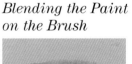

Too dry.

Too much water.

Correct.

3 As you start moving the brush, gradually start releasing the pressure. As you continue to make the stroke, do not allow the chisel of the brush to pivot at all. Continue pulling the comma toward you and gradually release pressure.

4 Now all the pressure should be off the brush and only the chisel of the brush will be touching the surface. Continue to pull toward yourself so the chisel creates the tail of the stroke. The brush chisel will end up being gradually lifted off the surface.

Left-Sided Comma Stroke

1 Set the chisel edge of your brush on the surface. Make sure to start your stroke with the chisel of the brush at the angle at which the stroke will end. Apply pressure to the bristles until you reach the bottom of the bounce. The bristles should lie smoothly to the side; they should not be squished out of shape.

2 As you start moving the brush into the curve of the stroke, start to gradually release the pressure on the bristles (remember, do not pivot the chisel edge of the brush). Continue slightly releasing pressure (lifting the brush) as you pull the stroke.

3 With all of the pressure off your brush, pull along the chisel edge of the brush to create the tail of the stroke.

Right-Sided S-Stroke

1 Turn your painting surface to the proper position, and set the chisel of the loaded brush at the angle that the stroke will end. Pull the brush, riding on the chisel edge (right-handed painters at five o'clock, left-handed painters at ten o'clock). Gradually add pressure to the brush while pulling the stroke to the side.

2 Continue adding pressure until you reach the bottom of the bounce. Hold at this pressure and pull through the middle of the stroke. Continuing to pull the stroke, start releasing the pressure on the brush.

3 Gradually release all pressure until you are pulling along the chisel of the brush (the stroke should end at five o'clock for right-handed painters, ten o'clock for left-handed painters).

Left-Sided S-Stroke

1 Turn the surface so you can start the stroke correctly (the stroke should end at two o'clock for right-handed painters and seven o'clock for left-handed painters). Set the chisel of the brush on the surface and pull without applying pressure. Gradually apply pressure as you pull the stroke to the side.

2 Continue adding pressure to the brush until you reach the bottom of the bounce and pull the stroke further.

3 Continue pulling the stroke while releasing pressure (remember not to pivot your brush). Release all pressure and complete the stroke by pulling along the chisel edge of the brush (the tails of the stroke will run parallel to each other).

Line Stroke

1 Begin pulling the stroke to create a line (with no pressure on the brush), and lean the brush handle forward very slightly in the opposite direction you are pulling the stroke.

2 Continue pulling along the chisel of the brush, keeping the brush handle in the same position as in step one. Do not apply any pressure to the brush at any time while making line strokes.

3 Continue pulling the line stroke to the end (as long as needed), then lift the brush off the surface.

Flat Stroke

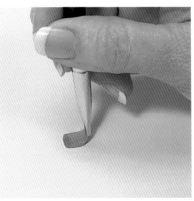

1 Apply pressure to the brush until you reach the bottom of the bounce. The pressure should be applied *before* you start moving the brush.

2 Begin moving the brush while maintaining continuous pressure.

3 Continue pulling the stroke in a straight line while holding the pressure evenly. When you reach the desired length of the stroke, release the pressure and lift the brush off the surface.

U-Strokes

1 Set the chisel of the brush onto the surface (the chisel should be facing at twelve o'clock). Pull the chisel toward yourself while applying no pressure.

2 Gradually add pressure to the brush while laying the bristles to the side to start creating the curve. (Right-handed painters pull the stroke from left to right. Left-handed painters pull the stroke from right to left.) Continue adding pressure to the brush until you reach the bottom of the bounce. Continue pulling the stroke to the side while slowly releasing pressure.

3 With all the pressure released on the brush, slide the chisel of the brush up and away from you at the twelve o'clock position (the tails of the stroke will run parallel to each other).

Upside-Down U-Stroke

1 With the brush handle straight up-and-down, set the chisel of the brush onto the surface of the painting (the chisel should be facing twelve o'clock). Push the brush away from yourself to create a tail on the stroke without adding pressure to the brush.

2 Start adding pressure to the brush while pushing into the curve of the stroke (as with the U-stroke, right-handed painters make the stroke from left to right, left-handed painters make the stroke from right to left). Continue adding pressure until you reach the bottom of the bounce. Start releasing the pressure while beginning to pull the stroke back toward yourself.

3 Releasing all pressure on the brush, pull the stroke along the chisel toward yourself to create the other tail of the stroke.

Top Half Circle Stroke

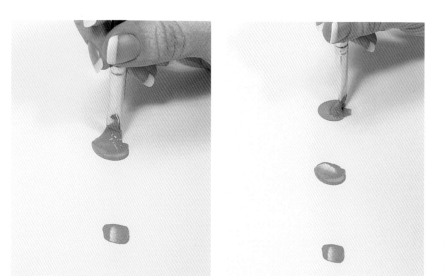

1 With the brush handle straight up-and-down, lay the chisel edge of your brush onto the surface and apply pressure to the bottom of the bounce, laying the bristles away from yourself.

2 While holding the pressure on the brush, begin pivoting the chisel of the brush so that the handle begins rolling in your fingers. (Right-handed painters roll from left to right, left-handed painters roll from right to left.)

3 Continue to hold the pressure and rotate the brush until you reach the end of the half circle point (the chisel will begin and end at two o'clock for right-handed painters and ten o'clock for left-handed painters).

Bottom Half Circle Stroke

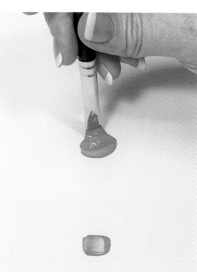

1 With the brush handle straight up-and-down, lay the chisel of the brush at the angle that the stroke will end. Apply pressure until you reach the bottom of the bounce with the bristles lying toward you.

2 While holding the pressure steady on the brush, begin pivoting the chisel edge, rolling the handle in your fingers (right-handed painters pivot the chisel of the brush from left to right, left-handed painters pivot from right to left).

3 Continue to hold the pressure and pivot the brush until you reach the half circle point (the stroke stops when the chisel edge is at five o'clock for right-handed painters and seven o'clock for the left-handed painters).

Right Half Heart Stroke

1 With the brush handle straight up, set the chisel of the brush at the center line of the stroke. Apply pressure on the brush to the bottom of the bounce (chisel at two o'clock). Begin to pivot, maintaining pressure on the brush (right-handed painters pull from left to right at two o'clock, and left-handed painters paint stroke from right to left at ten o'clock).

2 Continue to pivot the brush about two-thirds of the way through the stroke. At this point start gradually releasing the pressure on the brush while continuing to pivot.

3 Release all pressure (by this time you will be back at the center line of the stroke), and pull the tail of the stroke along the chisel edge of the brush.

Left Half Heart Stroke

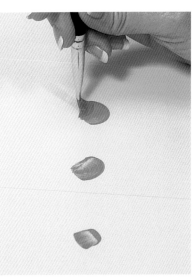

1 Keeping the brush handle straight up-and-down, lay the chisel of the brush at five o'clock for right-handed painters and ten o'clock for left-handed painters. Apply pressure to the brush until you reach the bottom of the bounce.

2 While continuing to hold the pressure, pivot the brush (right-handed painters pull the stroke from left to right, left-handed painters pull from right to left). Continuing to pivot brush about two-thirds of the way through the stroke. At this point, gradually start releasing the pressure on the brush while continuing to pivot.

3 Releasing all pressure (by this time you will be back at the center of the stroke), pull the chisel edge of the brush to create the tail of the stroke.

Right Half Leaf Stroke

1 Set the chisel of the brush at the center line of the stroke. Keeping the brush handle straight up-and-down, apply pressure to the brush until you reach the bottom of the bounce. Begin pivoting the brush while holding the pressure (right-handed painters pivot brush from left to right, left-handed painters from right to left).

2 Continue to hold pressure and pivot while slightly lifting pressure off the brush. Continuing to pivot the brush, push back into the pressure to create a small bulge in the leaf.

3 Smoothly release pressure while continuing to pivot until you reach the center of the leaf stroke, then with no pressure on the chisel of the brush, pull the tail of the stroke.

Left Half Leaf Stroke

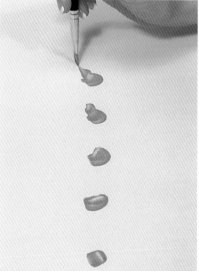

1 Begin with the brush handle straight up-and-down. Place the chisel edge of the bristles against the center line of the stroke, and apply pressure on the bristles until you reach the bottom of the bounce. Continuing pressure, begin to pivot the brush (letting the brush roll between your fingers).

2 Continue pivoting the brush while slightly lifting about one-half of the pressure. Continuing to pivot the brush, add pressure to push a bulge into the half leaf stroke.

3 Continue pivoting while releasing pressure until you reach the center line of the leaf. With no pressure, pull the chisel of the brush along the center line to create the tail of the stroke.

Crescent Stroke

1 With the brush handle straight up-and-down and the chisel on the surface, slide along the chisel edge (the tails of this stroke will angle toward each other).

2 Pivot the brush slightly and add pressure into the curve of the stroke (right-handed painters make the stroke from the left to the right, left-handed painters make the stroke from right to left). Continue adding pressure until you reach the bottom of the bounce while pulling the stroke to the side (out and away from your body) with a slight pivot.

3 Begin releasing pressure while continuing to slightly pivot the brush. Releasing all pressure on the brush, pull the tail of the stroke along the chisel edge of the brush, angling slightly toward the first tail of the stroke. The crescent stroke differs from the U-stroke as follows:
- The brush needs to pivot slightly to create the stroke. In the U-stroke, there is no pivoting.
- The tails of the crescent stroke angle toward each other while the tails are parallel with the U-stroke.

Double Crescent Stroke

1 As with the crescent stroke, begin with the brush handle straight up-and-down, and push the brush (without pressure) along the chisel edge to create the tail (all steps of this stroke continually pivot slightly).

2 Begin adding pressure to the brush while pulling into the first curve of the stroke. While holding the pressure on the brush, push into the dip in the middle of the stroke.

3 Begin to release pressure on the brush and create the second curve of the stroke. Releasing all pressure, pull the brush along the chisel edge to create the second tail (the tails of this stroke, like the crescent stroke, will angle toward each other).

CHAPTER 5

Double-Loaded Brush Strokes

How to Load the Brush

1 With the chisel edge of your brush straight, lay the handle parallel to the palette and lightly dip half of the chisel edge into White. Turn the brush over so that the White is facing up; dip the clean edge into Black Cherry.

2 Before blending, check your brush. Each color should cover about one-half of the chisel edge of the brush and slightly meet in the middle.

3 With the brush handle straight up-and-down, apply pressure to the brush on the palette paper. Holding the pressure on the brush, pull a small track—about 1-inch (25mm)—to begin blending the paint colors together.

4 Flip the brush over, lay the brush down onto the palette with the dark paint loaded edge next to the previously blended track (dark paint to dark paint). Apply pressure to start blending the paint on the other side of the brush.

Repeat steps 1 through 4 several times to get enough paint on the brush. Each time you reload the brush, try to reblend in the same paint track previously used to help build paint on the brush.

5 After blending the colors, check the brush; one side should still be straight White, one side Black Cherry, and the center should be a gradual blend of the two colors.

Blending the Paint on the Brush

Under blended.   Over blended.   Correctly blended.

Right-Sided Comma Stroke

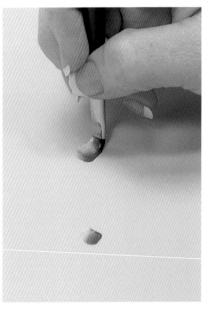

1 Lay the chisel of the brush at the angle you will end the stroke (right-handed painters at five o'clock, left-handed painters at ten o'clock). It helps to visualize a filbert brush as if it were a flat brush. In your mind put the corners back on the brush. This will help you know when the brush is positioned properly to begin and end the various strokes. When I refer in the instructions to place the chisel edge of the brush at a certain angle, do so if it were a flat brush (with corners).

2 Apply pressure to the bristles of the brush until you reach the bottom of the bounce.

3 As you begin moving your brush into the stroke, gradually release the pressure on the brush.

4 Continue pulling the stroke and releasing pressure.

5 Releasing all pressure on the brush, pull the tail of the stroke along on the chisel of the brush.

Left-Sided Comma Stroke

1 Set the chisel of the brush at the angle that the stroke will end (right-handed painters at two o'clock, left-handed painters at seven o'clock). Remember to visualize the chisel of the brush as if it were a flat brush.

2 Apply pressure to the brush until you reach the bottom of the bounce. You will not be moving the brush yet, only applying more pressure.

3 Gradually release pressure and pull the brush into the curve of the stroke.

4 Continue releasing pressure while moving the brush out and away from your body.

5 With all pressure released, pull along the chisel of the stroke to create the tail.

Line Stroke

1 With the brush handle straight up-and-down, set the brush lightly on the surface. Do not add any pressure to the brush. Lean the brush handle very slightly in the opposite direction that you are pulling the stroke.

2 Pull the stroke along the chisel of the brush, keeping the brush handle at the same angle as step 1.

3 Continue to pull along on the chisel of the brush as long as needed to complete the stroke.

Flat Stroke

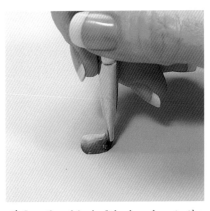

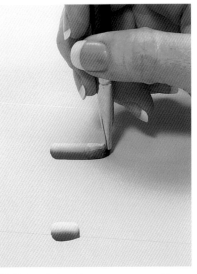

1 Lay the chisel of the brush onto the painting surface. Keep the handle of the brush straight up-and-down while applying pressure until you reach the bottom of the bounce.

2 Maintaining the pressure on the brush, begin pulling the stroke.

3 Continue pulling the stroke, maintaining even pressure on the brush for the desired length of the stroke.

Right Sided S-Stroke

1 Set the chisel of the brush on the painting surface with the brush handle straight up-and-down. Pull along the chisel of the brush to create the beginning tail of the stroke (no pressure at this step).

2 Begin adding pressure while pulling the stroke to the side.

3 Continue adding pressure to the brush until you have reached the bottom of the bounce. While holding the pressure, pull the middle of the stroke.

4 Continue pulling the stroke while you begin to release the pressure on the brush.

5 Releasing all the pressure on the brush, pull the tail of the stroke by riding along the chisel of the brush (the tails of the S-stroke will be parallel to each other).

Left-Sided S-Stroke

1 Lightly set the chisel edge of the brush onto the surface at the angle you want the stroke to end (keep the brush handle straight up-and-down). Pull along the chisel to create the first tail of the stroke.

2 Gradually add pressure while pulling the stroke to the side.

3 Continue adding pressure until you reach the bottom of the bounce. Pull to create the center of the stroke.

4 Begin to release pressure while continuing to pull the stroke.

5 Release all pressure and pull along the chisel of the brush to create the end tail of the stroke (the tails are parallel to each other).

U-Strokes

1 With your brush handle straight up-and-down, set the chisel of your brush onto the surface and pull without adding pressure (right-handed painters pull stroke from left to right, left-handed painters pull stroke from right to left).

2 Begin adding pressure to the brush pulling into the curve of the stroke.

3 Add pressure until you reach the bottom of the bounce and pull through the halfway point of the stroke.

4 Begin releasing the pressure while starting to push the bristles away from yourself.

5 Releasing all the pressure on the brush, push along the chisel, keeping the tails of the stroke parallel to each other.

Upside-Down U-Stroke

1 With no pressure on the brush, set the chisel of the brush on your surface at the angle you will end the stroke and push away to create the first tail of the stroke.

2 Begin adding pressure gradually as you start pulling the stroke to the side (right-handed painters pull stroke from left to right, left-handed painters pull stroke from right to left).

3 Continue adding pressure as you pull the stroke to the side until you reach the the bottom of the bounce. Hold the pressure through the middle of the stroke.

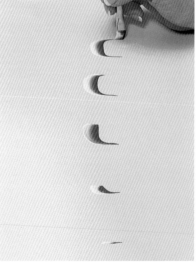

4 Begin to gradually release the pressure while pulling into the curve of the stroke.

5 With all pressure released from the brush, pull the tail of the stroke along the chisel of the brush, keeping the tails of the stroke parallel.

Crescent Stroke

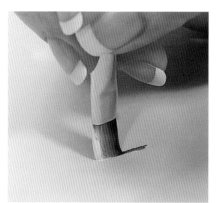

1 With the brush handle straight up-and-down, set the chisel of the brush on the surface. Push to create the first tail of the stroke without adding pressure to the brush.

2 Gradually add pressure, pulling the stroke to the side while slightly pivoting the chisel of the brush.

3 Add pressure until you reach the bottom of the bounce. Continue to pull through the middle of the stroke while slightly pivoting the chisel of the brush.

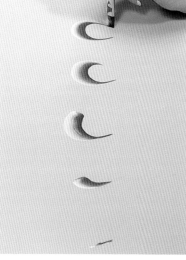

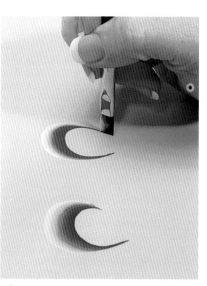

4 Continuing to slightly pivot the chisel of the brush, begin to release the pressure while pulling the stroke toward the second tail.

5 Releasing all pressure on the brush, continue to slightly pivot the brush while pulling along the chisel of the brush to create the second tail (the tails will angle toward each other).

6 Finished stroke, close-up.

Double Crescent Stroke

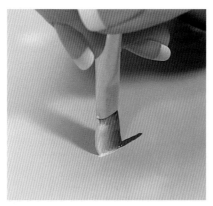

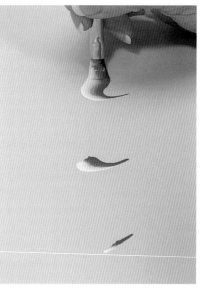

1 With the brush handle straight up-and-down, rest the chisel on the surface without adding pressure, and push along the chisel to create the first tail of the stroke.

2 Begin adding pressure while pushing to the side (right-handed painters pull stroke from the left to the right, left-handed painters from right to left), pivoting slightly.

3 Adding pressure until you reach the bottom of the bounce, push into the curve of the stroke while continuing to pivot.

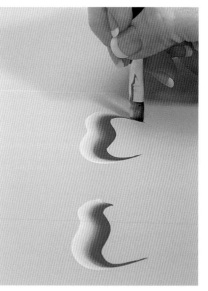

4 Begin releasing the pressure, pushing in and out of the curves and heading toward the tail of the stroke. Make sure to continue pivoting slightly at each step.

5 Releasing all pressure and riding along the chisel of the brush, create the second tail of the stroke (the tails will angle toward each other).

6 Finished stroke, close-up

Top Half Circle Stroke

1 With the handle of your brush straight up-and-down, set the chisel of the brush onto the painting surface and apply pressure until you reach the bottom of the bounce with the handle of the brush facing away from yourself.

2 Holding the pressure on the brush, pivot the brush by rolling the handle in your fingers (right-handed painters pivot the brush from left to right, left-handed painters pivot from right to left).

3 Continue holding even pressure on the brush while pivoting until you reach the half circle point. Make sure the pivoting corner of the brush stays in place while the outside corner travels all the way around the half circle point (for right-handed painters, the chisel should end at two o'clock, for left-handed painters, ten o'clock).

Bottom Half Circle Stroke

1 With the brush handle straight up-and-down, apply pressure to the surface beginning with the chisel at the angle you want the stroke to end. When applying the pressure to the brush, lay the bristles where the handle is toward you (right-handed painters, the chisel will be at five o'clock, left-handed painters, seven o'clock).

2 Holding even pressure on the brush, begin pivoting the brush with the leading edge rolling toward yourself (right-handed painters pivot the stroke from left to right, left-handed painters from right to left).

3 Continue to pivot while holding the pressure until the chisel of your brush is at the same angle that you began the stroke, making a half circle.

Right-Sided Half Heart Stroke (Pivoting Stroke)

1 Begin this stroke by laying the chisel edge at the angle you will end the stroke (right-handed painters at two o'clock, left-handed painters at seven o'clock). Add pressure until you reach the bottom of the bounce.

2 Holding the pressure of the brush, begin pivoting as for a half circle stroke.

3 Continue holding pressure and pivoting about two-thirds of the way through the stroke.

4 Continuing to pivot, begin releasing the pressure and start pulling the stroke toward the tail.

5 Releasing all pressure, pull the tail of the stroke by pulling along the chisel edge as you reach the halfway point.

6 Finished stroke, close-up.

Left-Sided Half Heart Stroke

1 Keeping the brush handle straight up-and-down, set the chisel of the brush at the angle you want to end the stroke (right-handed painters at five o'clock, left-handed painters at ten o'clock). Apply pressure to the brush until you reach the bottom of the bounce.

2 Continuing to hold pressure on the brush, begin to pivot the outside edge of the chisel of your brush (right-handed painters pull the stroke from left to right, left-handed painters pull from right to left).

3 Continue to hold the pressure and pivot the brush about two-thirds of the way through the stroke.

4 Gradually release pressure on the brush while continuing to pivot and pull down toward the tail.

5 Gradually release all pressure on the brush and drag down the brush on its chiseled edge to create the tail.

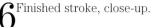

6 Finished stroke, close-up.

Right-Sided Half Leaf Stroke

1 Set the chisel of the brush at the center line of the stroke. Make sure the chisel is set at the angle that the stroke will end. Apply pressure until you reach the bottom of the bounce, keeping your brush handle straight up-and-down.

2 Maintaining pressure on the brush, begin pivoting (right-handed painters pull stroke from left to right, left-handed painters pull stroke from right to left).

3 Continue pivoting the brush while slightly lifting off the pressure.

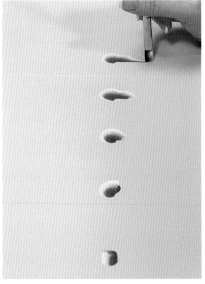

4 Continue pivoting the brush and push back into the small bulge in the leaf stroke.

5 Gradually release all pressure while continuing to pivot the brush until you reach the half leaf point. Pull along the chisel edge to create the tail of the stroke.

Left-Sided Half Leaf Stroke

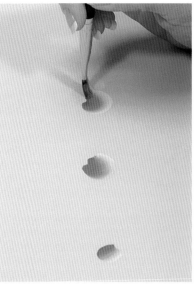

1 With the brush handle straight up-and-down, place the chisel of the brush onto the surface at the angle you will end the stroke. Apply pressure on the bristles until you reach the bottom of the bounce.

2 Maintaining the pressure on the brush, begin pivoting as for the half round stroke.

3 Continue to pivot the brush while you start lifting the pressure.

4 Continue to pivot the brush while pushing back into the pressure to create a bulge in the leaf stroke.

5 Continue pivoting the brush while gradually releasing all pressure. Pull along the chisel edge to create the tail of the stroke.

6 Finished stroke, close-up.

CHAPTER 6

Tipped Brush Strokes

How to Load the Brush

1 Squeeze fresh White paint onto your wet palette. Load a round brush by applying pressure on the bristles while pulling a track of paint out from the puddle.

2 Flip the brush completely over and load the other side of the brush. You will be loading the round brush as if it were a flat brush. With the brush handle straight up-and-down, tap the tip of the brush on a dry paper towel to remove some of the paint.

3 Slightly dip the tip of the brush in the Black Cherry paint (puddle squeezed onto the wet palette).

4 Pick up a small amount of Black Cherry (as you continue to reload your brush and make more strokes, work to stay consistent in the amount of paint on the tip of your brush).

5 Apply pressure once on your palette paper (not the wet palette), keeping your brush handle straight up-and-down. Flip the brush completely over and apply pressure once to the other side of the brush. Do not blend any more.

Blending Paint on the Brush

Under blended.

Over blended.

Correctly blended.

Right-Sided Comma Stroke

1 With the brush handle straight up-and-down, set the chisel of the brush (visualize this round brush as if it were a flat brush) at the angle you will end the stroke. Apply pressure to the brush until you reach the bottom of the bounce.

2 Gradually release pressure on the brush while pulling the stroke (right-handed painters pull at five o'clock, left-handed painters pull at ten o'clock). Continue pulling the stroke while releasing pressure (remember, do not pivot the brush).

3 Releasing all pressure on the brush, pull the tail of the stroke along the chisel of the brush.

Left-Sided Comma Stroke

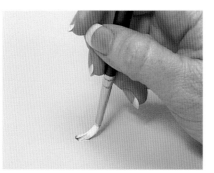

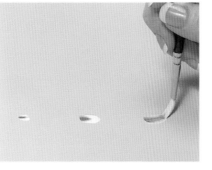

2 Gradually begin releasing pressure on the brush while moving into the curve of the stroke. Continue releasing pressure and pulling into the stroke without pivoting the brush.

1 With the brush handle straight up-and-down, set the flattened chisel of the brush at the angle you will end the stroke (right-handed painters pull at two o'clock, left-handed painters at seven o'clock). Apply pressure without moving the brush until you reach the bottom of the bounce.

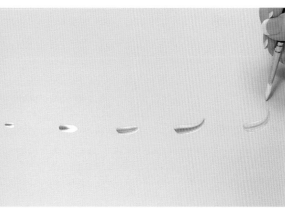

3 Release all pressure on the brush and pull the tail of the stroke along the chisel edge of the brush.

Line Stroke

1 Set the chisel of the brush onto the surface with the brush handle straight up-and-down. Do not apply any pressure during this stroke.

2 Very slightly tip the handle in the opposite direction that you are pulling the stroke. It will likely be most comfortable for right-handed painters to pull the stroke toward two o'clock or five o'clock, left-handed painter at ten o'clock or seven o'clock.

3 Continue pulling the stroke without adding pressure for the desired length of the line.

Flat Stroke

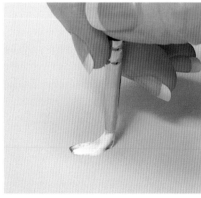

1 Apply pressure to the brush until you reach the bottom of the bounce. Apply full pressure *before* you begin to pull the brush.

2 Maintain even pressure while moving the brush into the stroke. The goal of this stroke is to keep the width of the stroke even (you can do this by holding the pressure before and while you are moving the brush).

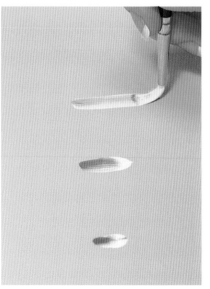

3 Continue maintaining pressure while pulling the stroke for the desired length.

Right-Sided S-Stroke

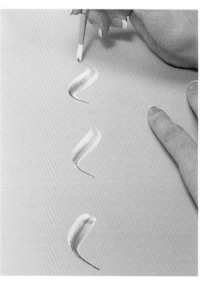

1 Set the chisel edge of the brush (as if it were a flat brush) onto the surface with the brush handle straight up-and-down. Do not apply pressure. Pull to create the first tail of the stroke (face the chisel of the brush at five o'clock for right-handed painters, ten o'clock for left-handed painters).

2 Begin adding pressure to the brush while pushing to the side. This will start opening up the brush (do not pivot the brush). Apply pressure while continuing to push into the stroke until you reach the bottom of the bounce. Begin lifting the pressure off the brush while pulling toward the tail of the stroke.

3 Releasing all pressure, pull the second tail of the stroke along the chisel edge of the brush (the tails of the stroke will be parallel to each other).

Left-Sided S-Stroke

1 With the brush handle straight up-and-down, set the chisel of the brush onto the surface at the angle you want the stroke to end (check the clock). Pull to create the first tail of the stroke without adding pressure.

2 Gradually add pressure while pushing to the side into the stroke. Continue adding pressure until you reach the bottom of the bounce. Hold through the middle of the stroke.

3 Gradually release pressure on the brush while beginning to pull the stroke toward the tail. Releasing all pressure, pull the second tail of the stroke parallel to the first tail along the chisel of the brush.

U-Stroke

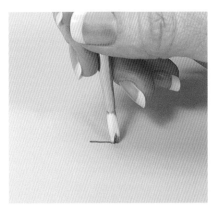

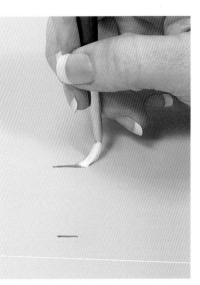

1 With the brush handle straight up-and-down, set the chisel of the brush onto the surface. Pull along the chisel toward yourself, without adding pressure, to create the first tail of the stroke (right-handed painters make the stroke from left to right, left-handed painters from right to left).

2 Begin adding pressure to the bristles while pushing the chisel toward the side.

3 Continue to add pressure on the bristles until you reach the bottom of the bounce while pushing through the center of the stroke.

4 Begin to release pressure on the brush, and allow the chisel to push up and away, aiming toward the second tail of the stroke.

5 Releasing all pressure from the brush, slide the brush to create the second tail of the stroke, which will be parallel to the first one.

Upside-Down U-Stroke

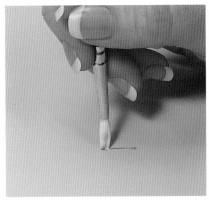

1 Keeping the handle of the brush straight up-and-down, set the chisel of the brush at the angle you will end the stroke (refer to the clock). As with the U-stroke, make the stroke out and away from your body. Push the brush away from yourself to make the first tail of the stroke.

2 Gradually add pressure as you push the bristles out and to the side.

3 Add pressure until you reach the bottom of the bounce. Continue to push through the center of the stroke.

4 Continue pushing into the stroke while beginning to release pressure from the brush. Aim toward the tail.

5 Releasing all pressure, pull along the chisel edge of the brush to create the second tail (parallel to the first).

Top Half Circle Stroke

1 With the handle of your brush straight up-and-down (visualize the chisel as if it were a flat brush), lay the chisel at the angle you will end the stroke. The bristles will face toward yourself with the handle facing away (right-handed painters pivot the stroke from left to right at two o'clock, left-handed painters, right to left at ten o'clock).

2 Apply pressure until you reach the bottom of the bounce. Continue holding even pressure on the brush while pivoting until you reach the half circle point. Make sure the pivoting corner of the brush stays in place while the outside corner travels all the way around the half circle point (for right-handed painters, the chisel should end at two o'clock, for left-handed painters, ten o'clock).

3 Continue pivoting and holding pressure until you reach the half circle point.

Bottom Half Circle Stroke

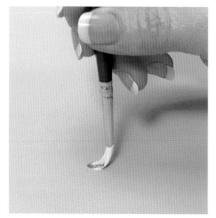 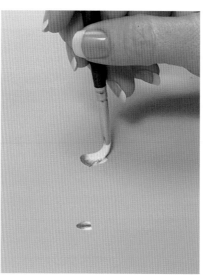 

1 Keeping the brush handle straight up-and-down, set the chisel edge at the angle you will end the stroke. Apply pressure with the chisel of the brush facing away from yourself and the handle toward yourself.

2 Holding even pressure, begin pivoting the chisel with the outer edge rolling toward yourself (right-handed painters from left to right at five o'clock, left-handed painters from right to left at seven o'clock).

3 Continue holding pressure and pivoting until you reach the half circle point.

The Complete Book of Basic Brushstrokes for Decorative Painters

Right-Sided Half Heart Stroke

1 Set the chisel of the brush at the angle you will end the stroke. Apply pressure until you reach the bottom of the bounce.

2 Maintain the pressure on the brush and begin to pivot the outer edge of the chisel as with the half circle. Continue pivoting with pressure about two-thirds of the way through the stroke.

3 Continue pivoting while beginning to release pressure on the brush. Release all pressure while pulling along the chisel edge to create the tail of the stroke.

Left-Sided Half Heart Stroke

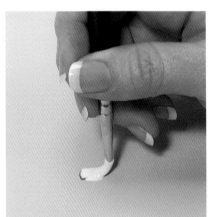

1 Holding the brush handle straight up-and-down, set the chisel of the brush at the angle you will end the stroke (right-handed painters pivot the stroke from left to right at five o'clock, left-handed painters from right to left at ten o'clock). Apply pressure to the bottom of the bounce.

2 Hold the brush and begin pivoting. Continue pivoting the brush while holding even pressure (about two-thirds of the way through the stroke).

3 While still pivoting the brush, begin releasing the pressure and pulling toward the tail of the stroke. Releasing all pressure, pull the tail of the stroke along the chisel edge of the brush.

Right-Sided Half Leaf Stroke

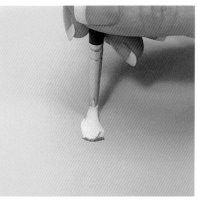

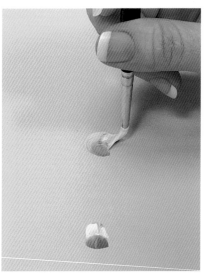

1 Set the chisel of the brush at the angle you will end the stroke, and apply pressure until you reach the bottom of the bounce.

2 Holding the pressure on the brush, begin pivoting the outer edge of the chisel.

3 Continue to pivot and begin to release a little of the pressure on the brush.

4 Continue pivoting the brush and push back into the pressure to create a small bulge.

5 Continuing to pivot the brush, release all pressure and pull the brush along the chisel edge to create the tail.

Left-Sided Half Leaf Stroke

1 Place the chisel edge of the brush at the angle you will end the stroke (right-handed painters pull the stroke from left to right at five o'clock, left-handed painters pull from right to left at ten o'clock). Keep the brush handle straight up-and-down. Apply pressure until you reach the bottom of the bounce.

2 Hold the pressure and begin pivoting the brush, letting the brush roll in your fingers.

3 Continue pivoting the brush while slightly lifting off some of the pressure.

4 Press back into the pressure on the brush while continuing to pivot. Pull slightly toward the tail of the stroke.

5 Release all pressure and pull the tail of the stroke along the chisel edge of the brush.

Crescent Stroke

1 Set the chisel of the brush on the surface with the handle straight up-and-down. Begin the stroke by sliding along the chisel edge without adding pressure.

2 Pivot the brush slightly while adding some pressure, and pull into the curve of the stroke.

3 Continuing to pivot slightly. Add pressure until you reach the bottom of the bounce, and push through the center of the stroke.

4 Keep pivoting and begin to release some pressure on the brush, angling toward the tail of the stroke.

5 Release all pressure on the brush while continuing to slightly pivot. Pull along the chisel edge of the brush to pull the tail (the tails will angle toward each other).

Double Crescent Stroke

1 With the brush handle straight up-and-down, set the chisel of the brush onto the surface and, without adding pressure, slide along the chisel to create the first tail of the stroke.

2 Continue to pivot slightly while adding pressure to the brush, pushing into the curve of the stroke.

3 Add pressure until you reach the bottom of the bounce, then push into the dip in the middle of the stroke (continue pivoting).

4 Gradually release pressure on the brush and create the second curve of the stroke (continue pivoting).

5 Release all pressure on the brush. While you continue to pivot the brush, pull along the chisel of the brush to create the tail (the tails will angle toward one another).

CHAPTER 7

Side-Loaded Brush Strokes

How to Load Your Brush

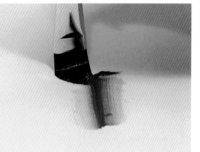

1 Lay the handle of the damp brush parallel to your painting surface with the chisel of the brush straight up-and-down. Dip the long corner of the brush into the paint puddle (the paint should be on your wet palette).

2 With the brush handle straight up-and-down, begin blending the paint slightly across the brush on your acrylic palette paper.

3 Flip your brush over. Set the loaded chisel of the brush paint to paint on the acrylic palette and stroke to blend. The paint will gradually fade across the brush without reaching the other edge of the brush. You will see one sharp edge of the stroke but not see the other.

Blending the Paint on the Brush

Under blended.　　　Over blended.　　　Correctly blended.

Right-Sided Comma Stroke

1 Set the chisel of the ½-inch (12mm) angle brush in the direction the stroke will end. For the angle brush, you will not have the handle straight up-and-down; instead, keep the handle at the angle that will make the entire chisel of the brush evenly rest on the surface. Apply pressure until you reach the bottom of the bounce. All this is done before you begin to move the brush.

2 Begin slightly releasing the pressure on the brush as you start moving into the stroke (check the clock for pulling angle). Continue pulling the comma while gradually releasing pressure on the brush. You will begin to see a strong edge of green paint on one side, fading to clear on the other. If color appears on the side that should be clear, you have blended the paint too far across the brush.

3 Continue pulling the stroke, gradually releasing pressure on the brush (remember, do not pivot on these strokes). Then, releasing all the pressure on the brush, with the entire chisel evenly against the surface, pull along the chisel to create the tail of the stroke.

Left-Sided Comma Stroke

1 Set the entire chisel of the brush against the painting surface evenly (the brush handle will be at an angle). Make sure the chisel of the brush is at the angle the stroke will end.

2 Apply pressure evenly on the bristles until you reach the bottom of the bounce. You are not moving the brush yet, only applying pressure. Begin slightly releasing pressure as you start moving the brush (if you are moving the brush, you must be releasing pressure).

3 Continue gradually releasing pressure while moving the brush into the stroke. Releasing all pressure on the brush and keeping the entire chisel on the surface, pull the brush to create the tail of the stroke. Remember to keep the chisel of the brush at the same angle throughout the stroke.

Flat Stroke

1 With the brush handle straight up-and-down, apply pressure to the bristles of the brush until you reach the bottom of the bounce.

2 Maintain pressure on the bristles while moving the brush straight into the stroke.

3 Continue holding the pressure, and pull the stroke for the desired length before lifting pressure off the brush.

Right-Sided S-Stroke

1 Keep the handle of the brush at an angle to allow the entire chisel of the brush to rest on the painting surface. Set the chisel down at the angle you wish the stroke to end (right-handed painters at five o'clock, left-handed at ten o'clock). Pull slightly to create the first tail of the stroke without adding pressure to the brush.

2 Gradually add pressure to the brush while pulling the stroke to the side. Continue applying pressure until you reach the bottom of the bounce, and pull through the middle of the stroke.

3 As you move into the stroke, begin releasing the pressure on the brush. Keep the chisel edge parallel to the first tail. Releasing all pressure on the brush, pull along the chisel edge to create the second tail.

Left-Sided S-Stroke

1 Keep the brush handle at the angle that will allow the entire chisel to lay evenly against the surface. Maintain this brush position throughout the entire stroke. Set the chisel of the brush at the angle you want to end the stroke (right-handed painters at two o'clock, left-handed painters at seven o'clock). Pull the brush without adding pressure to create the first tail.

2 Gradually add pressure to the chisel of the brush while pulling the stroke to the side. Continue adding pressure and pulling the stroke until you reach the bottom of the bounce. Pull the stroke through the middle area of the S-stroke.

3 Begin releasing pressure on the brush while pulling the stroke toward the tail. Then, releasing all pressure on the brush, pull to the second tail by riding along the full chisel edge of the brush. The tails of the stroke will be parallel to each other.

U-Stroke

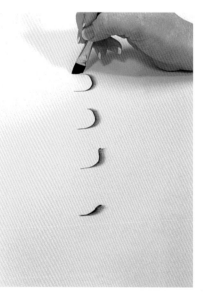

1 Keep the brush handle at the angle that will allow the entire chisel end to rest evenly on the surface (right-handed painters pull the stroke from left to right, left-handed painters pull from right to left). Pull along the chisel edge to create the first tail of the stroke.

2 Gradually add pressure as you pull the stroke toward yourself, pushing to the side. Apply pressure while pulling the brush through the middle of the stroke. At this point, the pressure will be at the bottom of the bounce.

3 Begin releasing the pressure, pushing the stroke toward the second tail. Release all the pressure on the brush, keeping the entire chisel against the surface. With no pressure, push up and away to create the second tail. The tails will be parallel to each other.

Upside-Down U-Stroke

1 Keep the brush at an angle so that the chisel edge of the brush is evenly against the surface. Adding no pressure to the chisel, slide the chisel up and away to create the first tail.

2 Begin adding pressure as you push the stroke sideways. Continue adding pressure as you push through the middle of the stroke.

3 Gradually start releasing the pressure. Aim the chisel of the brush toward the second tail of the stroke (tails will be parallel). Release all pressure on the brush while keeping the entire chisel of the brush even on your surface. Pull along the chisel edge to create the second tail of the stroke.

Top Half Circle Stroke

1 Lay the entire chisel edge at the angle you will end the stroke (right-handed painters pivot stroke from left to right, left-handed painters pivot from right to left). Apply pressure to the bristles until you reach the bottom of the bounce.

2 Maintaining pressure on the brush, begin pivoting with the long edge of the angle brush toward the outside. The long edge will move all the way around the outside of the stroke. The short edge pivots in place.

3 Continue to hold pressure and pivot until you reach the half circle point, then lift your brush.

The Complete Book of Basic Brushstrokes for Decorative Painters

Bottom Half Circle Stroke

1 With the brush handle at an angle, place the entire chisel of the brush at the angle you will end the stroke (check the clock).

2 Holding even pressure on the brush, begin pivoting. Keep the short end of the chisel pivoting in place to help avoid making a rainbow-type stroke (unless you want to learn rainbows—then just add them to your practicing!).

3 Continue to hold pressure and pivot until you reach the half circle point, then lift your brush.

Right-Sided Half Heart

For the half heart and half leaf I found it easier to load the shorter edge of the chisel blender rather than the longer end as in the other side-loaded strokes. Remember not to allow the paint to blend all the way across the brush. You should only see where the paint begins, not ends.

1 Keep the brush handle at the angle that will allow the entire chisel of the brush to set evenly on the surface, with the chisel in the direction you will end the stroke. In this case, the short edge of the chisel will be toward the outside so it travels around the edge of the stroke. The long edge of the angle blender will pivot in place. Apply pressure evenly on the bristles until you reach the bottom of the bounce.

2 Holding consistent pressure on the brush, begin pivoting the shorter edge of the angled chisel. Continue holding pressure while pivoting the brush about two-thirds of the way through the stroke.

3 Continue pivoting while gradually releasing pressure and pulling the brush toward the tail of the stroke. Release all pressure and pull along the chisel to create the tail. The entire chisel will remain evenly against the surface in all the steps for this stroke.

Left-Sided Half Heart

1 Set the chisel of the brush against the surface at the angle you will end the stroke (right-handed painters angle toward five o'clock, left-handed painters toward ten o'clock). Apply even pressure until you reach the bottom of the bounce.

2 Keep even pressure on the brush and begin pivoting the shorter edge of the angle blender. Continue holding pressure and pivoting the brush for about two-thirds of the way through the stroke.

3 Continue pivoting the brush while gradually releasing the pressure on the brush. Pull the brush toward the tail of the stroke. Gradually release all pressure on the brush, and pull the tail along the chisel of the bristles.

Right-Sided Half Leaf Stroke

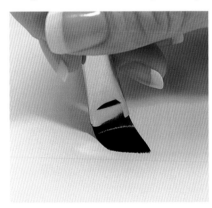

1 Set the chisel of the brush on the surface at the angle the stroke will end (right-handed painters at two o'clock, left-handed painters at seven o'clock). Apply pressure until you reach the bottom of the bounce.

2 While holding pressure on the brush, begin pivoting with the short edge of the angle brush traveling around the outside of the stroke. Continue to pivot the brush while lifting some of the pressure off the brush.

3 Continuing to pivot, add pressure back into the brush to create a small bulge in the stroke. Gradually release pressure again while continuing to pivot. Pull the stroke toward the tail. Releasing all pressure, pull the tail along the chisel of the brush.

Left-Sided Half Leaf Stroke

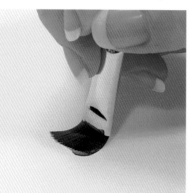

1 Set the entire chisel of the brush onto the painting surface at the angle the stroke will end (right-handed painters at five o'clock, left-handed at ten o'clock). Apply pressure until you reach the bottom of the bounce.

2 Holding pressure on the brush, begin pivoting the shorter end of the brush (the edge loaded with paint). Continue pivoting the brush while letting off some of the pressure.

3 Continue pivoting the brush. Push back into the pressure to create a small bulge in the stroke. Gradually release pressure while continuing to pivot the brush and pulling toward the tail of the stroke. Release all pressure and pull to create the tail of the stroke along the chisel of the brush.

Crescent Stroke

1 Set the entire chisel of the angle brush onto the surface. Line up the stroke so you will end the stroke at five o'clock for right-handed painters, seven o'clock for left-handed painters. Push the chisel to create the first tail of the stroke without adding pressure.

2 Begin adding pressure while slightly pivoting the brush, and push the stroke to the side.

3 While continuing to gradually pivot the brush, add pressure until you reach the bottom of the bounce. Pull through the middle of the stroke.

4 Continuing to slightly pivot the brush, begin releasing pressure and pulling toward the tail of the stroke.

5 Release all pressure on the brush, creating the tail of the stroke by pulling along the chisel edge. The tails will angle toward each other.

Double Crescent

1 As with the crescent stroke, set the chisel of the brush onto the surface. Line up to make sure the stroke will end in your most comfortable position (five or seven o'clock). Without adding pressure, push along the chisel of the brush to create the first tail of the stroke.

2 Gradually add pressure to the brush while slightly pivoting and pushing to the side. Continue slightly pivoting, adding pressure until you reach the bottom of the bounce. Pull toward the dip in the stroke.

3 Holding pressure, push into and out of the dip of the stroke while continuing to slightly pivot your brush. Gradually release pressure on the brush. Come out of the dip and pull toward the tail of the stroke. Releasing all pressure, pull along the chisel to create the tail. The tails of the stroke will not be parallel, but will angle toward each other.

Linework

Loading the Brush

1 Using a no. 0 script liner, add equal parts water to your paint.

2 Thoroughly mix together the paint and water.

3 Lay the loaded brush onto an absorbent paper towel. Roll to remove all excess water and paint from the metal ferrule and bristles.

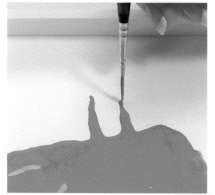

4 Hold the brush handle to its side, and lay the hairs of the brush into the paint puddle. Using pressure, roll the bristles out from the puddle, keeping pressure on the tips of the bristles (this will give you the feel of a full fountain pen). If the paint does not have enough water, your linework will tend to drag or skip. If you mix too much water, your linework will be transparent and fuzzy.

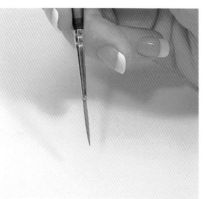

5 Hold the brush handle straight up-and-down and put pressure only on the tip of the brush.

Loops Linework

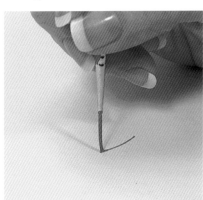

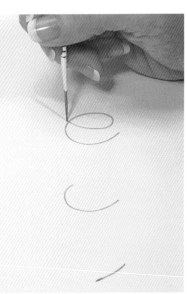

1 Keeping the brush handle (no. 0 script liner) straight up-and-down, lightly touch the tip of the brush to the surface. Maintain the same light pressure, and start moving your hand and the brush in a large circular motion.

2 Continue to move in a circle, maintaining the same brush angle and pressure (right-handed painters move from left to right, left-handed painters move from right to left). Allow your hand (which is resting on the table) to slide with the circular motion. (The movement is actually a shoulder motion.)

3 Continue to add loops all in one stroke until you run out of paint in your brush.

Figure Eights Linework

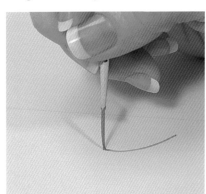

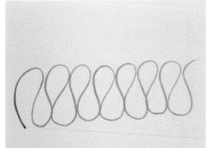

1 Get into a comfortable position. With the handle of the brush straight up-and-down, lightly touch the tip of the liner brush to the surface. Begin figure eights by making a curved line away from yourself.

2 Keep the tip of the brush on the surface, and pull into a loop and back toward yourself, curving in the opposite direction. Repeat this motion, back and forth.

3 Continue to create figure eight lines that overlap each other. Remember that the keys to good linework are loading the brush correctly, holding the brush at the correct angle and the amount of pressure put on the brush tip.

Small S Linework

1 Holding the brush straight up-and-down, set the tip of the brush down and stroke up and to the right while lifting the brush off the surface.

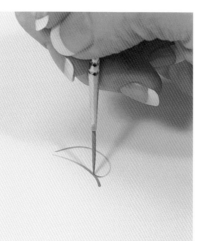

2 Set the brush down where the last stroke left off. Pull toward yourself and curve in an S-shape back toward the beginning of step 1.

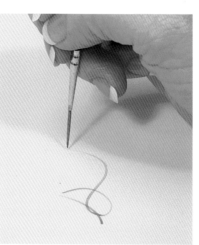

3 Create a loop at the base of the small S. Do not pick up the brush, just continue to make the next S. Repeat steps 1 through 3 several times until your brush runs out of paint.

Scribbles Linework

1 Scribbles are very random, so go for it. Just play! Start with some big curves.

2 Make figure eights (large or small).

3 Make loops and other random combinations of curves.

Border Variations

Script liner (S-strokes and lines), round (comma strokes).

Liner (comma strokes), stylus (dip-dots and dip-dot hearts).

Flat (side-loaded upside down U-strokes), stylus (dip-dots).

Liner (stems), angle shader (leaves), stylus (small dip-dot flowers), large stylus (large dip-dot flowers).

Liner (S-strokes and lines).

Script liner (linework), angle shader (leaves), stylus (dip-dot flowers).

Script liner (stems), angle shader (flowers and buds), stylus (dip-dot baby's breath).

Angle shader (flowers and buds), round (leaves), liner (stems).

Angle shader (leaves with white flowers), chisel blender (pink flowers), liner (stems and tendrils), stylus (dip-dot flower centers).

Script liner (S-strokes and lines), round (comma strokes), stylus (dip-dots).

The Complete Book of Basic Brushstrokes for Decorative Painters

Border Variations

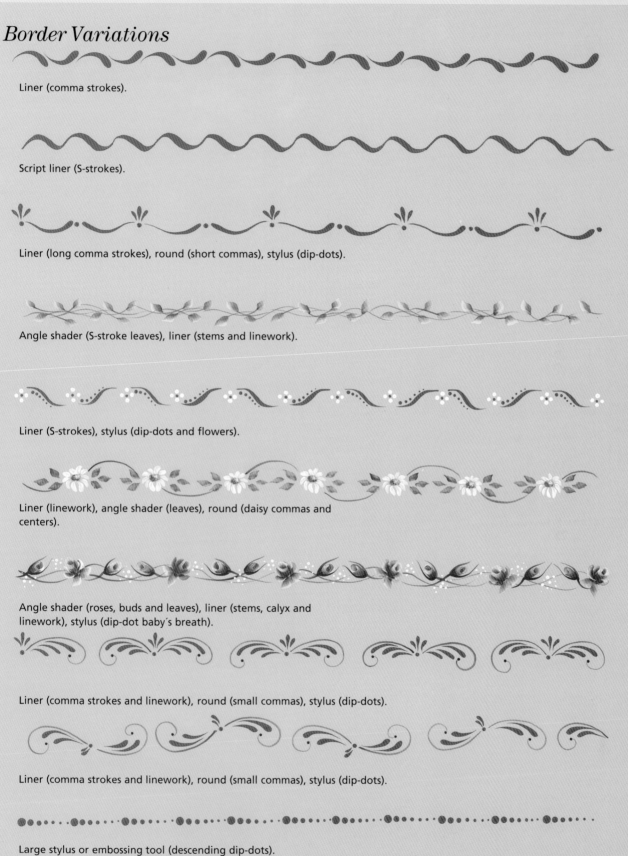

Liner (comma strokes).

Script liner (S-strokes).

Liner (long comma strokes), round (short commas), stylus (dip-dots).

Angle shader (S-stroke leaves), liner (stems and linework).

Liner (S-strokes), stylus (dip-dots and flowers).

Liner (linework), angle shader (leaves), round (daisy commas and centers).

Angle shader (roses, buds and leaves), liner (stems, calyx and linework), stylus (dip-dot baby's breath).

Liner (comma strokes and linework), round (small commas), stylus (dip-dots).

Liner (comma strokes and linework), round (small commas), stylus (dip-dots).

Large stylus or embossing tool (descending dip-dots).

Border Variations

Script liner (interlocking S-strokes).

Liner (comma strokes), round (small commas), script liner (linework), stylus (dip-dots).

Liner (S-strokes), stylus (dip-dots), large stylus or embossing tool (dip-dot hearts).

Liner (comma strokes), stylus (descending dip-dots).

Liner (comma and S-strokes), stylus (dip-dot hearts).

Liner (comma strokes), round (small comma strokes), stylus (dip-dots).

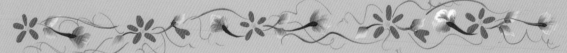

Liner (comma strokes) script liner (linework), stylus (dip-dots).

Angle shader (double-loaded flowers and leaves), liner (touch lift flowers and tendrils), script liner (stems and lines), stylus (flower centers).

Liner (touch lift white flowers), angle shader (leaves), script liner (linework), stylus (dip-dots and hearts).

Script liner (linework), liner (holly leaves fill-in), large stylus (descending dip-dots).

Border Variations

Round (leaves), stylus (dip-dot flowers and hearts).

Round (leaves), liner (linework), stylus (dip-dot flowers).

Liner (comma strokes and straight commas), stylus (dip-dots).

Liner (S-strokes).

Liner (S-strokes), stylus (descending dip-dots).

Liner (comma strokes), stylus (dip-dots).

Angle shader (S-stroke leaves), liner (linework), stylus (dip-dots and hearts).

Angle shader (S-stroke leaves), liner (linework), stylus (dip-dot-pull flowers).

Liner (comma strokes and straight commas), stylus (dip-dots).

Angle shader (S-stroke leaves), script liner (stems), stylus (dip-dots).

PROJECT 1

Daisy Striped Box

Daises are such cheerful flowers! They are beautiful and simplistic. They are also perfect to start putting all that practice on our comma strokes into action. Start by laying out and practicing the single-layer daisy. Then practice the double-layer daisy.

This small oval bentwood box is a perfect place to store special memories, photos, letters and other treasured momentos.

The daisy box has many different techniques to work with–the actual daisies, a simple S-stroke border, the stripes on the box–that will make the painting complete.

When transferring on the pattern for the daisy, it is best not to transfer on the individual comma strokes; instead, draw (or transfer) an oval to represent the outer edge of the flower and offset the oval to represent the center of the flower. Draw lines to divide the daisy into quarters. Start painting the flower, pulling commas from the front center, turning your flower to the position that you can pull the strokes more comfortably. You will most likely have to turn the flower several times to pull the strokes at the most comfortable angle.

MATERIALS

- no. 2 round
- no. 6 flat
- no. 10/0 liner
- ¾-inch (19mm) Aqua Tip

Surface: Small bentwood box, available from

Valhalla Designs
343 Twin Pines Dr.
Glendale, OR 97442
Phone/fax: (541) 832-3260

Chambray Blue

Tide Pool Blue

Silver Pine

Pine Green

Light Ivory

Butter Yellow

Burnt Sienna

Black

Top of lid.

Side of box.

These patterns may be hand-traced or photocopied for personal use only. Enlarge at 118 percent to bring up to full size.

The Complete Book of Basic Brushstrokes for Decorative Painters

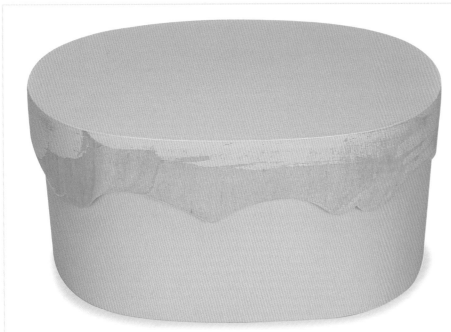

1 Basecoat the top of the lid and the entire box with Chambray Blue (inside and out, bottom also). Use a ¾-inch (19mm) Aqua Tip brush.

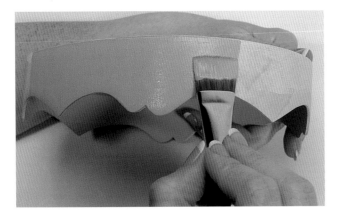

2 Using a ¾-inch (19mm) flat brush, basecoat the sides of the lid with Tide Pool Blue. Brushstrokes need to be applied in the same direction. If needed, wait until the first base coat is dry and apply a second coat.

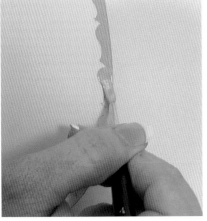

3 Trace the pattern for daisies, leaves and stroke edge. Transfer the entire pattern to the box lid. Using a no. 2 round, basecoat (using an S-stroke motion) the outside border edge of the lid top (repeat if needed for full coverage).

4 Continue the previous step until you have a frame all the way around the lid.

5 Start the painting with a "shaky" half leaf stroke. Lay the edge of the flat brush at the base of the leaf and apply pressure. Pivot the brush slightly, then release half of the pressure. Continue to pivot the brush and apply pressure again. Repeat this process several times, slightly pivoting the brush each time.

6 Continue to pivot the brush, applying pressure and letting up on the pressure until you reach the end of the half leaf stroke. When the chisel of the brush is even with the end of the half leaf stroke, release all pressure on the brush and pull on the chisel of the brush to create the tail of the stroke.

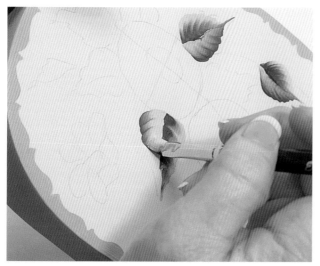

7 To paint the other side of the leaf, lay the chisel of the brush at the base of the other half of the leaf and repeat step 5 in the opposite direction. (Do not flip the brush over. You want the colors to go from dark to light, dark to light.)

8 Continue to pivot. Repeat step 6 in the opposite direction.

9 Begin the daisy by pulling single-loaded comma strokes (with Light Ivory and a no. 2 round brush) in the front of the daisy. These strokes should be longer in the front and gradually get shorter as the strokes move around to the back. Pull the strokes to fill the front right quarter of the daisy.

10 Pull the comma strokes to fill the back right quarter of the daisy (these strokes are much shorter).

11 Pull the comma strokes, filling the front left quarter of the daisy.

12 Pull the comma strokes to fill the back left quarter of the daisy.

13 Starting at the front of the daisy again for the second layer of petals, begin pulling comma strokes on top and in between the first layer of petals. Make sure the petals are slightly shorter than the bottom petals. Pull the commas to fill the front right quarter (make sure they are slightly offset from the first layer). Continue filling commas in the back right quarter of the daisy.

14 Pull the top layer commas, filling the front left quarter and continuing to fill the back left quarter.

15 Pull the comma right, center and left to create the back-facing daisy.

16 Repeat the previous step on the second back-facing daisy.

17 Double-load a no. 6 flat brush with Silver Pine and Pine Green. Pull two or three small S-strokes at the base of the backward daisies.

18 Single-load a no. 6 flat brush with Butter Yellow. To start basecoating the daisy center, pull a U-stroke on one side of the center.

19 Pull an upside-down U-stroke on the other side of the daisy center. (This should fill the entire center; if not, add additional strokes.)

20 Side-load the no. 6 flat brush with Burnt Sienna, and stroke a half U-stroke on the bottom left area of the daisy center for a shade.

21 Load the tip of a no. 2 round brush with Light Ivory. Tap paint onto the area opposite the shade (upper right) for a textured highlight.

22 With a no. 10/0 liner brush, create a mixture of half water, half paint using Burnt Umber. Tap dots with the tip of the brush around the daisy center. The dots should vary in size, with some dots spilling onto the petals. These are the stamens of the flower. More should be seen in the front of the flower and very few toward the back.

23 Using your no. 10/0 liner, mix Pine Green with equal parts water. Scribble the tendrils.

24 Using your no. 10/0 liner, pull stems on flowers and leaves.

25 Using your no. 10/0 liner and Light Ivory, make S-strokes around the edge of the lid to create the border where the two colors of blue meet. Connect S-strokes with a short line.

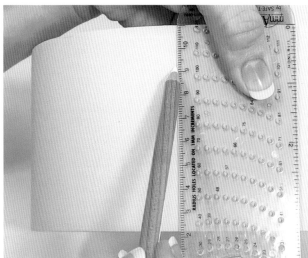

26 Using a ruler, draw a line onto the box with a white chalk pencil (make sure the line is at a right angle to the edges of the box).

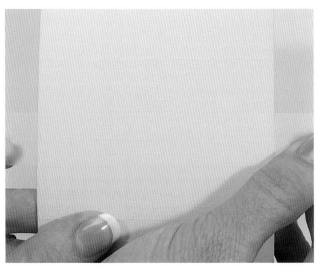

27 Apply tape with one edge against the line. Apply additional strips of tape against one edge of the previous strip, and continue adding strips of tape all the way around the box.

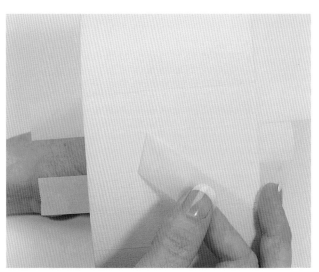

28 Remove every other strip of tape.

29 Using a Magic Rub Eraser, rub each edge of the tape strips firmly against the wood piece.

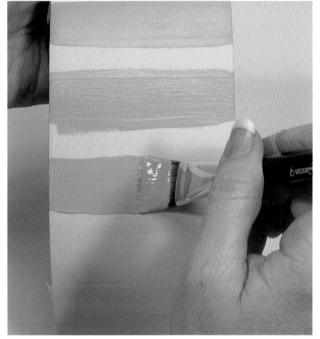

30 Using a ¾-inch (19mm) flat brush, basecoat the exposed stripes (repeat if necessary for complete coverage).

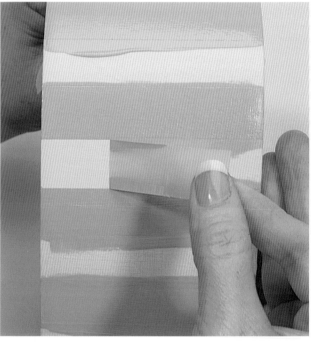

31 Remove the remaining tape carefully while the paint is still wet. Allow painted stripes to dry thoroughly.

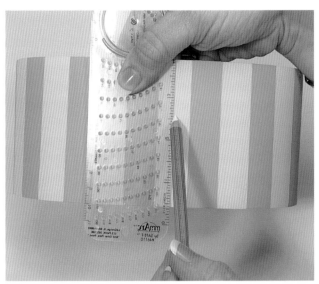

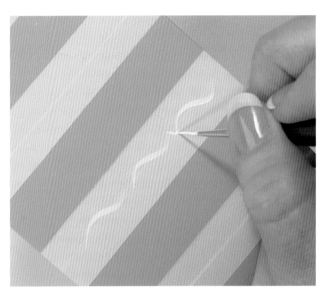

32 Using a ruler, draw a line down the center of the Chambray stripes with the white chalk pencil.

33 Using a no. 10/0 liner, make S-strokes along the white chalk lines on the Chambray stripes. Connect the tail of the S-strokes with short lines.

Finished box.

Running Roses Wall Sconce

One of the many wonderful things about decorative painting is the combination of beauty and usefulness. The wall sconce is quite beautiful without any decoration, but with the addition of these simple touches of color that create roses and leaves, it is now a piece of art that will look wonderful on any wall.

These little roses are a simple combination of U- and comma strokes. They may take a little time to learn, but once you have, you will be able to pop them on any surface to create a beautiful painting in minutes. Well worth the practice!

If you wish to have roses in other colors, double-load your brush with one light and one dark color, and make sure you will have enough contrast to see each individual petal. These roses look beautiful in all different colors; allow yourself to play.

Now best of all, if you have a blackout (like we had recently), you have a wonderful lamp to shed some light on an otherwise very dull evening.

MATERIALS

- no. 6 flat and no. 10 or no. 12 flat
- 5/0 script liner
- ¾-inch (19mm) Aqua Tip

Surface: Wall sconce with round lamp base available from

Western Woodworks
1142 Olive Branch Lane
San Jose, CA 95120
Phone/fax: (408) 997-2356

Blue Wisp

Rainforest

Mendocino Red

Oyster White

Deep River Green

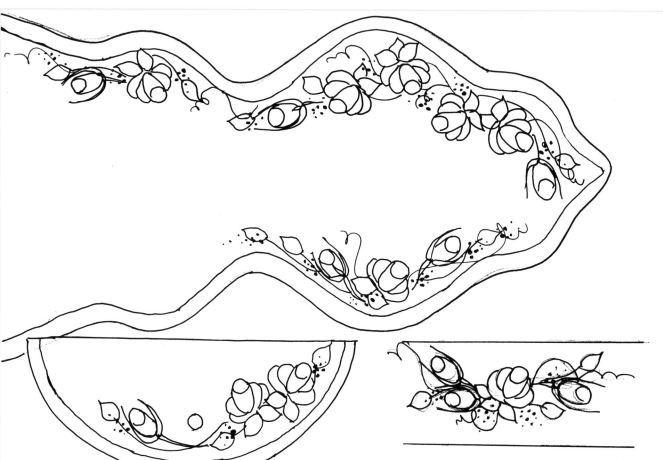

These patterns may be hand-traced or photocopied for personal use only. Enlarge at 166 percent to bring up to full size.

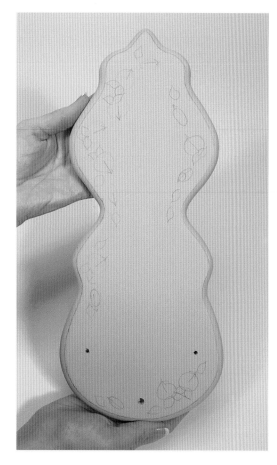

1 Sand the wood piece. Seal the wood piece. Sand again. Use a tack cloth to remove any dust.

Basecoat all the surfaces twice (more if needed for smooth, even coverage) with a ¾-inch (19mm) Aqua Tip brush.

Lightly matte spray the outside, if desired, two to three times. If matte spray is used, lightly rub #0000 steel wool over the surface.

Dust lightly with your tack cloth. Trace the entire pattern. Transfer roses and leaves to the surface.

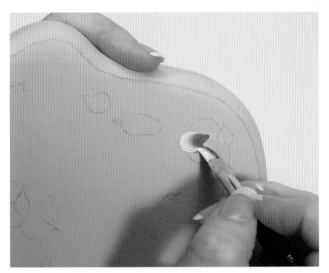

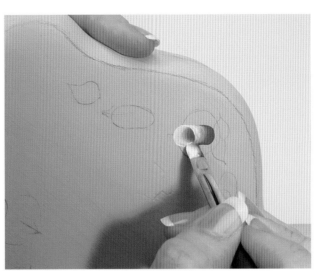

2 Using a double-loaded no. 6 flat brush (White and Mendocino Red), make an upside-down U-stroke with the White edge toward the outside. (You can put the Mendocino Red-loaded edge toward the outside. This also makes a beautiful rose, but you will need to be consistent with whichever color is toward the outside for all the strokes of the rose.)

3 To create the mouth of the rose, interlock a U-stroke on top of the previous stroke.

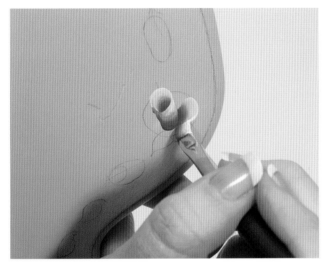

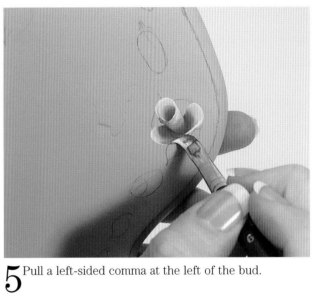

4 Pull a right-sided comma stroke at the side and bottom of the bud (created in the last two steps).

5 Pull a left-sided comma at the left of the bud.

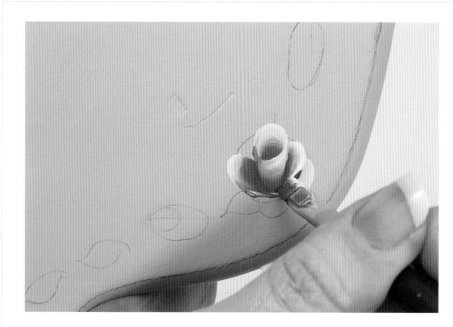

6 Lay the chisel of the brush against the edge of the bud. Adding pressure out and away from the bud, pull a smaller right-sided comma to fill the space between the bud (U-strokes) and the previous comma.

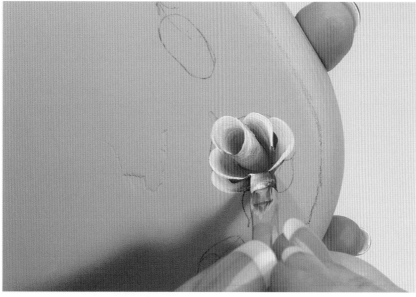

7 Repeat the previous step with a small left-sided comma.

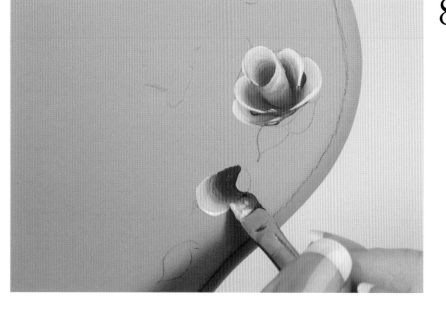

8 To create a rosebud, make an upside-down U-stroke.

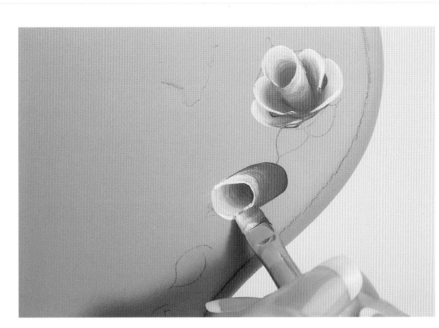

9 Interlock a U-stroke, overlapping the previous step (if you have a hole in the center when this step is completed, apply more pressure when pushing into your U-strokes).

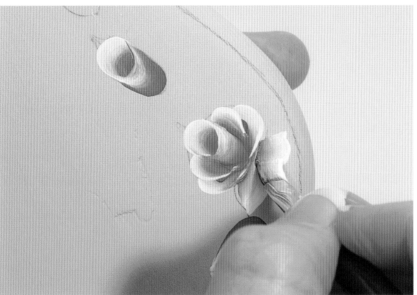

10 Double-load a no. 6 flat brush with Pine Green and White. Pull small S-strokes (both left and right) for leaves.

11 Load a no. 0 script liner brush in Pine Green.

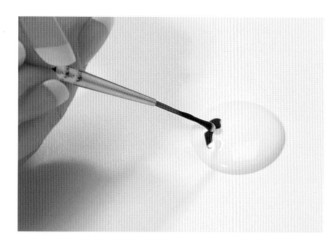

12 Lightly dip the tip of the brush in White (do not blend). The result of this loading style should be a small ball of white paint on the tip of the brush.

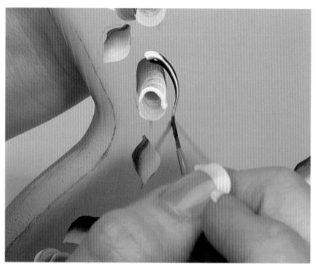

13 Place the tip of the brush at the base of the rosebud. Add pressure to the brush to deposit a small puddle, then pull up and release the pressure, creating a "puddle comma." This begins to create the calyx (the little leafy green thing at the base of the rosebud). Repeat a puddle comma on the other side of the rosebud and again at the base of the bud, creating the stem.

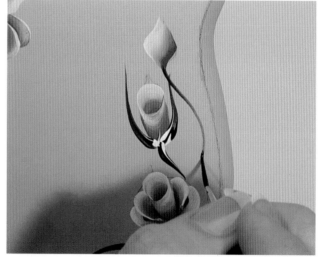

14 Mix one-half water to one-half Pine Green with your no. 0 script liner. With your brush handle straight up-and-down, use linework to attach leaves to flower groupings. These lines should be delicate and curvy. Don't make straight hard lines or it will be distracting to the overall look of your painting.

15 Using your no. 0 script liner, make random tendrils using scribble linework.

16 Using the large end of your stylus, dip into a fresh puddle of White paint. Touch your stylus onto the surface of your painting (without redipping into the paint) over and over again in a grouping until there is no paint left to create dots. This will give you several dot sizes in each group to give the appearance of baby's breath.

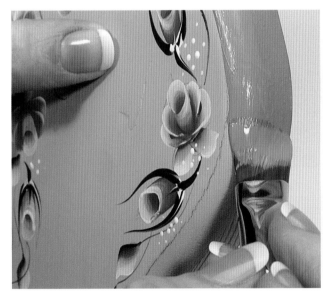

17 Using a no. 10 or no. 12 flat brush (smaller for the lamp base), basecoat the trim edges with Rainforest Green (this may need two coats to give full coverage). Allow to dry one to two days if possible. Apply three to four thin coats of varnish.

Completed wall sconce.

Wisteria Wastebasket

I have this beautiful ten-foot silk wisteria tree in my bedroom that I go to sleep and wake up under every night and day. It has such a wonderfully relaxing effect that I thought it would be great to design coordinated pieces for a master bathroom.

The piece I selected for this design is a wastebasket. Don't be limited to this piece; try adding a tissue box cover or a small jewelry box. Decorating with several coordinated pieces adds a professional touch to a room.

Wisteria is a light and lacy flower. The strokes are simple and repetitive to create these flowers. Keep some strokes transparent and others opaque (not see-through). The pattern for these flowers and leaves is random and loose to make the design look more natural and realistic.

MATERIALS

- no. 12 flat
- no. 8 flat
- ¾-inch (19mm) Aqua Tip filbert
- no. 0 script liner

Surface: Victorian wastebasket available from

Valhalla Designs
343 Twin Pines Dr.
Glendale, OR 97442
Phone/fax: (541) 832-3260

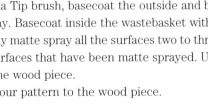

Chambray Blue

Wedgewood Blue

Purple

Pine Green

White

1 Sand the wood piece. Seal it, then sand again. Use a tack cloth to remove any dust.

With a ¾-inch (19mm) Aqua Tip brush, basecoat the outside and bottom of the wastebasket with Chambray. Basecoat inside the wastebasket with Wedgewood Blue. Allow to dry. Lightly matte spray all the surfaces two to three times. Rub #0000 steel wool on all surfaces that have been matte sprayed. Use a tack cloth to remove any dust on the wood piece.

Trace and lightly transfer your pattern to the wood piece.

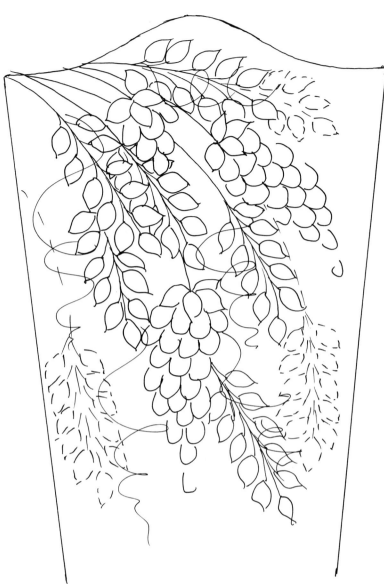

This pattern may be hand-traced or photocopied for personal use only. Enlarge at 200 percent to bring up to full size.

2 Load a no. 8 flat brush with Neutral Gel on your acrylic palette paper.

3 Brush mix Chambray and a touch of Pine Green (with the brush already loaded in Neutral Gel). This will be considered a single-loaded brush. The paint will be transparent because of the Neutral Gel.

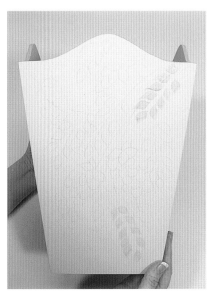

5 Continue transparent S-strokes. Wisteria leaves are made of a group of eleven small leaves on a stem. Finish all the transparent leaves.

4 Begin with small S-strokes to create the transparent leaves in the background.

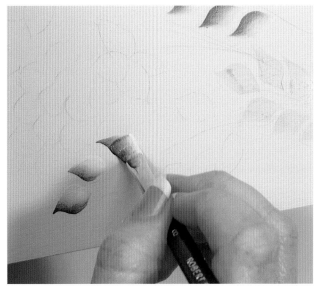

6 Continue to use the no. 8 flat brush loaded with Neutral Gel, Chambray and Pine Green. Riding on the chisel of the brush, create curved line strokes for the main stem that the leaves connect to. Pull small line strokes to connect the leaves to the main stem.

7 Load your no. 8 flat brush again with Neutral Gel, then double-load with White on one side and Pine Green on the other. Make small S-strokes to create the leaves in the foreground.

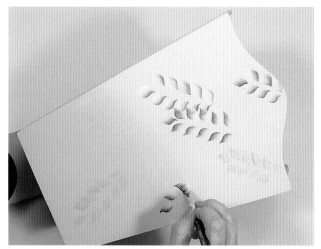

8 Continue making double-loaded S-strokes until all the leaves have been stroked.

9 With your brush still double-loaded, pull a long, curved line stroke for the main stem of the leaf grouping. Pull short line strokes to connect the leaves to the main stems.

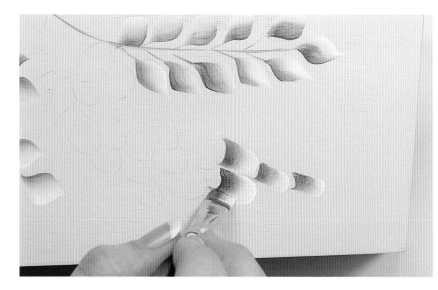

10 Load a no. 12 flat brush in Neutral Gel, then double-load the brush with Purple and White (if the color stems are too strong, add more Neutral Gel). Begin the wisteria by making small U-strokes at the bottom of the petal grouping.

11 Continue to make U-strokes (slightly bigger). Overlap the strokes to make the middle of the grouping.

12 Continue to make U-strokes to the top of the wisteria flowers.

13 Double-load your no. 8 flat brush as before for the leaves. Stroke small S-strokes to create the calyx on top of the wisteria, using the chisel of the brush to make a long line stroke for the stem of each flower.

14 Using a no. 0 script liner, scribble tendrils onto the painting. Erase all remaining transfer lines, and finish painting by varnishing all the surfaces.

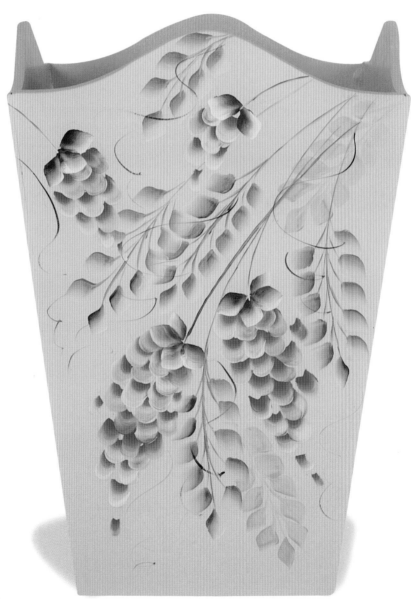

Completed wastebasket.

Poinsettia Tray

I always remember beautiful poinsettias around my mother's front door at Christmastime. They are so cheerful and warm, and they bring back wonderful memories of family, warm socks and hot cocoa. I wanted to reflect these feelings in the surface selected to paint.

The tray I selected reminded me of all those wonderful cookies we share with our family and friends during the holidays. I've used a medium-sized tray in this project, but they are also available in small, large, oval and round, so take your pick.

MATERIALS

- no. 2 and no. 8 flat
- ¾-inch (19mm) Aqua Tip
- no. 3 round
- no. 0 and no. 2 script liner

Surface: Hinderloopen round tray (large) available from

Valhalla Designs
343 Twin Pines Dr.
Glendale, OR 97442
Phone/fax: (541) 832-3260

Orange

Opaque Red

Black Cherry

Ivory

Silver Pine

Pine Green

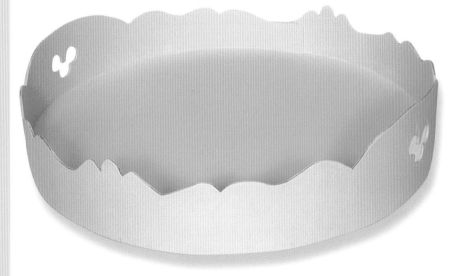

1 Sand the wood piece. Seal it and then sand again. Use a tack cloth to remove any dust.

Basecoat the wood surface with Ivory using your ¾-inch (19mm) Aqua Tip brush. After the piece is completely dry, take the project outside to a well-ventilated area and lightly matte spray two to three times. After the matte spray has dried, rub #0000 steel wool over the surface lightly. Use tack cloth to remove any steel dust.

Trace your pattern. Carefully line up the tracing to fit the design on the surface. Hold the tracing in place while you slowly slide the transfer paper between the pattern and wood piece. Using your stylus, lightly trace over the entire pattern, transferring the lines of the pattern onto your surface. Continue transferring until the entire pattern is on the wood piece. If the pattern appears too dark, lightly rub with a Magic Rub Eraser to lighten the transfer lines. Repeat the previous two steps to transfer the pattern onto the outside of the tray edge.

This pattern may be hand-traced or photocopied for personal use only. Enlarge at 170 percent to bring up to full size.

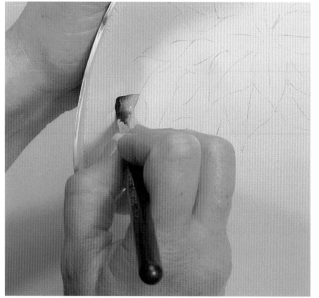

2 Double-load a no. 8 flat brush with Silver Pine and Pine Green. Beginning with the leaves farthest in the back, make a partial half heart stroke (this is used for the half leaf).

3 Repeat the previous step for the other side of the leaf.

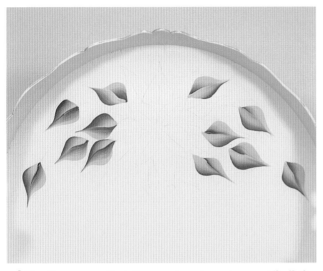

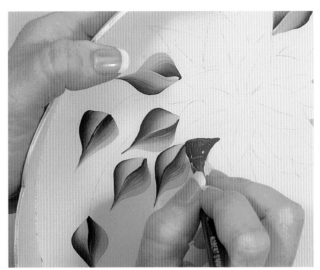

4 Continue repeating the previous two steps until all the leaves are in place.

5 Double-load your no. 8 flat with Opaque Red and Black Cherry, beginning with the poinsettia petals farthest back (there are three layers of petals). Make a partial half heart.

6 Repeat the previous step for the other side of the petal.

7 Continue to build poinsettia petals, back petals first, then the middle petals slightly overlapping onto the back petals.

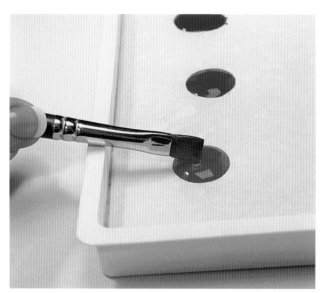

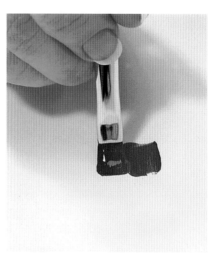

9 Lightly blend the triple-loaded brush on an acrylic palette.

8 Leaving the two previous colors blended on the no. 8 flat brush, side-load the Opaque Red side of the brush into the orange paint. This is called "triple loading."

10 Start the top four petals by stroking on a partial half heart stroke, creating half of the petal.

11 Repeat the previous step on the other side to make a complete petal.

12 Continue repeating the last two steps until all four top petals are complete (no background should show between the petals).

13 Using your no. 0 script liner, mix Pine Green paint and water (in equal proportions to an inklike consistency). With the brush handle straight up-and-down, pull linework stems from the leaves to the flower.

14 Continue pulling lines to connect all the leaves.

15 Using your no. 0 script liner, paint linework scribbles for tendrils.

16 Load the tip of a no. 2 round brush with Ivory. With the brush handle straight up-and-down, tap on a grouping of stamens at the center of the poinsettia.

17 Using a no. 3 script liner, load a damp brush with Opaque Red (do not water down the paint at this step; this is basecoating with a liner brush). Paint a line border where the bottom and edges of the tray meet. Measure from the base of the outside edge of the tray. Place tape on the upper outside edge (refer to page 82 for this technique), rub the bottom edge of the tape firmly with a Magic Rub Eraser to make sure the paint won't bleed under the tape. Paint the exposed bottom portion of the edge of the tray. Remove tape.

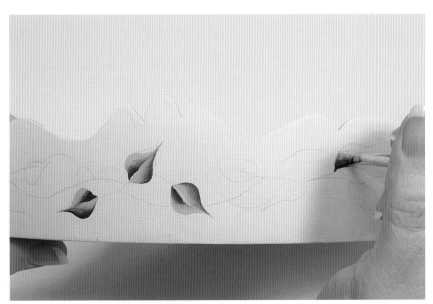 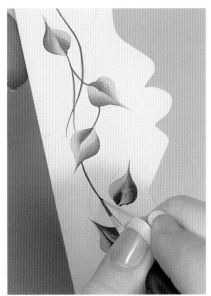

18 Double-load a no. 2 flat brush and stroke both right and left sides of the small leaves on the outside of the tray (these are the same leaves as used in the poinsettia pattern).

19 Using your no. 0 script liner, stroke linework connecting leaves and creating tendrils. After the painting is completely dry, apply three to five light coats of satin water-based varnish.

Completed tray.

Pansy Fan Box

Pansies are so beautiful and delicate; they come in an amazing array of colors and color combinations. Because they are color complements, the Yellow-and-Purple color combination is one of the most vibrant. Choosing a color combination can be difficult. There are so many different ways of painting them beautifully. After completing this project, try playing with some different color combinations using the same pattern.

This fan box is a great small jewelry or momento box. It also is perfect for adding a coordinated border around the box.

MATERIALS

- no. 8 flat
- ⅛-inch (3mm)
- ¼-inch (6mm) and ½-inch (12mm) angle brush
- no. 2 and no. 6 chisel blender
- no. 10/0 liner
- ¾-inch (19mm) Aqua Tip

Surface: Fan box (large) available from

Valhalla Designs
343 Twin Pines Dr.
Glendale, OR 97442
Phone/fax: (541) 832-3260

Buttercream

Opaque Yellow

Lavender Lace

Purple

Silver Pine

Pine Green

White

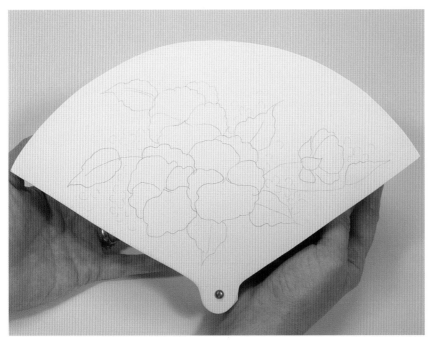

1 Sand the wood piece. Seal it, then sand again. Use a tack cloth to remove any dust.

Basecoat all surfaces of the fan box (top, bottom, sides, inside and outside). Optional: Lightly matte spray two to three times. Lightly rub the matte-sprayed surface with #0000 steel wool. Use a tack cloth to remove any steel dust.

Trace and transfer pattern to the wood piece.

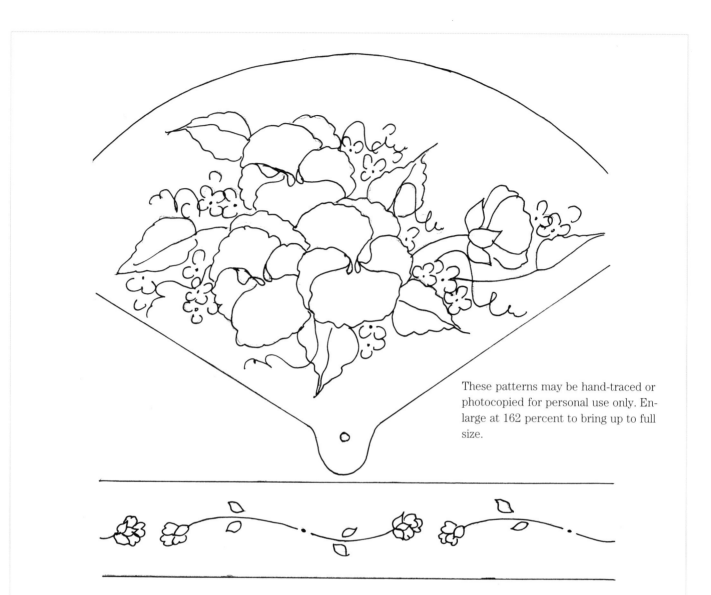

These patterns may be hand-traced or photocopied for personal use only. Enlarge at 162 percent to bring up to full size.

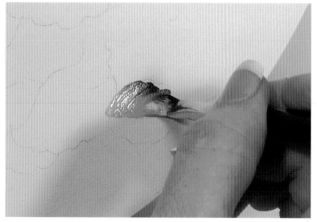

2 Double-load a no. 8 flat brush with Silver Pine and Pine Green. Begin a shaky half leaf stroke. (Remember to get in a comfortable position for the angle the stroke will end, not begin; right-handed painters at two o'clock, left-handed painters at seven o'clock.) Start the stroke by applying pressure until you reach the bottom of the bounce. Lift pressure and repeat while pivoting the chisel edge of the brush.

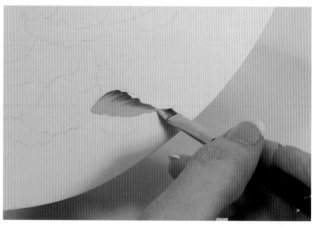

3 Continue pivoting the brush while repeatedly applying pressure and releasing pressure until you reach the end of the half leaf stroke. Then release all pressure, and pull the tail by riding along the chisel edge of the brush.

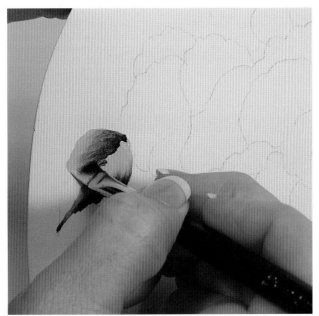

4 Repeat step 2 to make the other side of the leaf. Position the stroke to end for right-handed painters at five o'clock, left-handed painters at ten o'clock.

5 Repeat step 3 for the second half leaf stroke, ending with the two tails meeting at the tip of the leaf.

6 Double-load your ½-inch (12mm) angle brush with Lavender Lace on the long side of the chisel and Purple on the shorter side. Set the chisel of your brush at the edge of the petal and add pressure until you reach the bottom of the bounce. While gradually pivoting the brush, let up a little of the pressure, then push back into the pressure. While continuing this process, keep the short (Purple) edge of the chisel in place and allow the longer (lighter color) edge to travel to create the outer edge of the petal.

7 Continue the previous step for the other half of the stroke. This will end up being more like one-third of a circle.

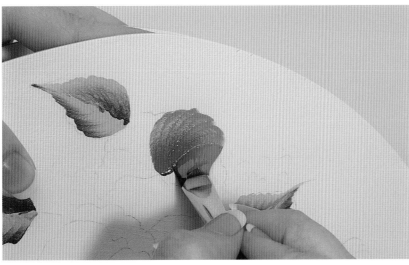

8 Allow step 7 to dry, then repeat steps 6 and 7 if the colors are too transparent. (Do this with each petal to keep the underneath petals from showing through the petals on the top.)

9 Repeat for the top purple petal, using the same technique.

10 This petal will be slightly offset from the first petal so you can see that they overlap. Repeat the last two steps if the petal is transparent.

11 After the purple petals are dry, reapply the pattern for the yellow petals. Load a clean ½-inch (12mm) angle brush with the long edge in Yellow and the short edge of the chisel in Purple. Set the chisel of the brush at the edge of the right front petal.

12 Apply pressure until you reach the bottom of the bounce, and begin pivoting while continually applying and releasing pressure, creating a shaky stroke. This petal will be narrower than the previous purple petals (the *end* of this stroke should be at five o'clock for right-handed painters and two o'clock for left-handed painters).

13 Turn your brush around so that in pulling the opposite side petal, you will end at two o'clock for right-handed painters and seven o'clock for left-handed painters. Repeat step 12.

14 Repeat step 11 on the front petal directly across from the previous yellow stroke.

15 Begin the large front yellow petal by overlapping onto the yellow side petals. This petal will be larger than the two side petals. You are still creating a pivoting half round stroke that is wiggly (applying and releasing pressure continually while pivoting the brush).

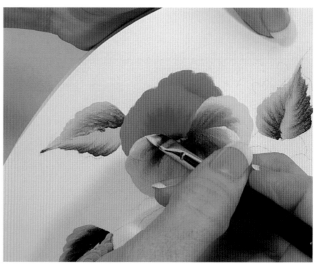

16 Continue with the shaky stroke, ending with the chisel edge overlapping onto the other yellow petal (right-handed painters pull this stroke from left to right, left-handed painters from right to left).

17 With your angle brush loaded as before for your double-loaded yellow and purple petals, set the chisel of the brush on the center upper edge of the petal on the front left.

18 Pull a tiny S-stroke to create a flip on the edge of the petal aiming toward the center of the flower.

19 Load the tip of a no. 10/0 liner brush with a tiny puddle of Light Ivory. Pull tiny commas at the center of the flower. The tails of the commas end at the edges of the side yellow strokes.

20 Dip the tip of your no. 10/0 liner brush in Silver Pine. Tap a tiny dot in the middle of the heads of the Light Ivory comma strokes to create the mouth of the flower. Repeat the previous strokes to create all three pansies. Work from the back petals forward.

21 Side-load a small chisel blender with Lavender Lace. Make small crescent strokes to create your filler flowers.

22 Load the tip of your no. 10/0 liner brush with a touch of Yellow, and tap centers of the filler flowers.

23 With your liner brush, mix one-half water and one-half Pine Green to an inklike consistency. Pull line-work stems connecting the leaves (slightly curve these lines).

24 Pull linework scribbles (pull tendrils from the flowers out and away from the design). Keep these light and random so they don't look stiff and attract too much attention.

25 Transfer the border design around the edge of the piece. Using a ⅛-inch (3mm) angle shader, double-load the brush with Lavender Lace on the longer end of the chisel edge and Purple on the shorter end. Make sure to keep the handle of the brush parallel to the palette paper while loading, or the single color of paint will easily go too far across the brush. Pull two tiny shaky pivoting strokes (just like the pansy petals on the top of the box).

26 Double-load a clean ⅛-inch (3mm) angle brush with Yellow and Purple. Pull shaky pivoting strokes overlapping onto the Purple strokes (the same as the petals for the large pansies).

27 With a clean ⅛-inch (3mm) angle brush, load the longer edge with Silver Pine and the shorter edge with Pine Green. Pull tiny S-strokes at the base of the flowers and on either side of the stems.

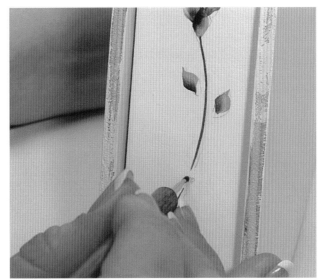

28 Using your no. 10/0 liner brush, mix Pine Green paint and water (equal parts) and pull linework for stems from the base of the flowers.

29 Using the larger end of your stylus, dip into fresh Pine Green, and paint a dot in between linework stems. After painting has dried a couple of days, apply several light coats of satin varnish to all surfaces.

Completed box.

Hydrangea and Roses Sewing Box

When I first saw this unique Victorian sewing box, I knew I had to paint it. Since there are so many surfaces to paint, I knew the painting as a whole would need to stay soft to not be overpowering.

This is one of those surfaces that you can really show a lot on. Big, beautiful roses seemed perfect—they are so popular, and everyone is drawn to them.

I selected hydrangea to fill in large areas so there would not be too much contrast. The entire design is kept in purples, mauves and blue to give an overall softness to a whitewashed background.

In fact, when you complete your painting, wash a little mauve or blue (mixed with Neutral Gel as described in the instructions) over small areas of the background and small areas with flowers and leaves to achieve an even softer appearance.

The rose leaves are made with wiggly half leaf strokes, while the hydrangea leaves are painted in slightly warmer colors and blended to make the piece more interesting.

This is another pattern that works well on surfaces of various sizes and shapes. A lazy Susan is a very easy (and impressive) piece to work on and shows off the design beautifully.

MATERIALS

- ¾-inch (19mm) Aqua Tip
- no. 8 flat
- no. 2 filbert
- no. 0 script liner
- ⅜-inch (10mm) angle
- no. 3 round

Surface: Victorian sewing box available from

Valhalla Designs
343 Twin Pines Dr.
Glendale, OR 97442
Phone/fax: (541) 832-3260

Purple	Purple Dusk	Lavender Lace	Dusty Mauve
Sachet Pink	White	Pine Green	Village Green
Butter Yellow	Salem Green	Silver Pine	

This pattern may be hand-traced or photocopied for personal use only. Enlarge at
125 percent to bring up to full size.

1 Sand all surfaces of the wood piece. Seal all surfaces. Sand all surfaces again. Use a tack cloth to remove any wood dust.

Mix White plus Neutral Gel (one-part paint, four-parts gel).

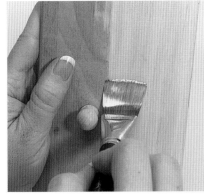

2 Apply paint mixture to the wood piece using a ¾-inch (19mm) angle shader brush. Stroking in the direction of the grain of the wood should result in a "stained" appearance as you stretch the paint onto the surface. Allow the surface to dry about eight to twelve hours.

Take your wood piece outside in a well-ventilated area and lightly matte spray two to three times. Allow to dry outside about thirty minutes. Rub #0000 steel wool over the entire surface. Use a tack cloth to lightly remove any steel dust remaining on the surface.

Trace and lightly transfer the pattern with dark transfer paper.

3 Begin hydrangea leaves by loading your brush with Neutral Gel, then double-load a no. 8 flat brush with Village Green and Pine Green. Start at the base of the leaf with a fairly large S-stroke. (The end of the S-stroke should be at the center of the leaf.) Continue to build S-strokes, gradually making them smaller and shorter as you pull strokes toward the tip of the leaf.

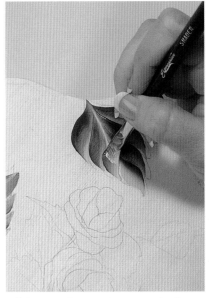

4 Repeat the previous step in the other direction for the other half of the leaf (it is best to begin S-strokes at the outside of the leaf and pull toward the center).

5 Without cleaning your brush, overstroke previous strokes. Slightly overlapping the edge of the strokes as you pull each overstroke will slightly blend the leaf for a softer look.

6 Repeat the previous step on the other side of the leaf, always blending toward the center of the leaf.

7 Load a no. 2 filbert brush first with Neutral Gel, then with Purple. Starting in the center of the hydrangea, lay the brush onto the surface, move your brush slightly and lift. Each tiny flower in the hydrangea has four petals and a tiny center. When creating the small flowers, the four petals will be stroked toward each tiny center. Continue to stroke on petals in groups of fours, overlapping them to start building a cluster. Turn the piece to keep a comfortable position.

8 Add more Neutral Gel to your already loaded brush (from the previous step) to make the petals more transparent. Continue building strokes in a larger area with the hydrangea.

9 Reload your no. 2 filbert with more Purple and load the tip of your brush in White. Press only one side of the brush onto your acrylic palette to slightly blend. Start stroking the individual petals on, as before, in the center of the existing Purple strokes. Reload in White, or first Purple, then White, as necessary for variety.

10 Repeat as needed to cover the center area (don't cover all the transparent purple petals).

11 Wipe your brush out with a paper towel (this is called working with a dirty brush), then load your brush with Purple Dusk. Tip in White and continue pulling petals in tiny groups of four in a larger area, slightly overlapping into the existing purple flowers.

12 Continue adding strokes in Purple Dusk tipped in White. Gradually add more Neutral Gel to the ones in the outer edges for the transparency, overlapping some petals onto the leaves.

13 Wipe your previously loaded no. 2 filbert on a paper towel, load your brush in Lavender Lace and tip in White. Stroke on petals of flowers overlapping onto the Purple Dusk petals and outward to create a larger flower area.

14 Continue adding strokes in Lavender Lace and White, gradually adding more Neutral Gel to create some transparent petals. These petals should extend to the outside edges of the hydrangea pattern. Do not overdo this step; you should be able to see lots of "air" (the background) through the outside edges of the flower.

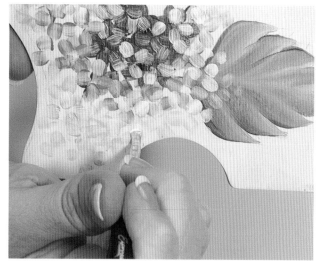

15 Wipe your brush out again. Load your brush in Sachet Pink and tip in White. Stroke petals overlapping onto the Lavender-Lace-and-White petals.

16 Add more Neutral Gel to your already loaded brush and continue to stroke petals very loosely at and over the outside edges of the flower. Try not to form a hard edge with an abrupt stop; instead have the petals get farther and farther apart so the edge looks airy.

17 Using the tip of a no. 3 round brush, load in Butter Yellow and tap on the centers of the many small flowers that make up the hydrangea.

18 Begin rose leaves by double-loading your choice of a no. 8 flat or a ⅜-inch (10mm) angle brush with Silver Pine and Salem Green. Working from the wide base of the leaf, stroke a shaky half leaf on the left. Start the stroke with pressure, slightly pivot and release half the pressure, then continue the pivot and add pressure.

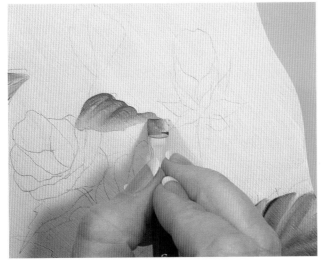

19 Continue pivoting while releasing pressure and adding pressure until the stroke comes to the center vein line of the leaf. Release all the pressure and pull the chisel of the brush to create the half leaf.

20 Repeat step 18 for the right side of the leaf (reload brushes as needed).

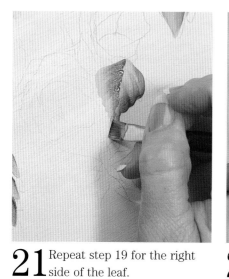

21 Repeat step 19 for the right side of the leaf.

22 Repeat steps 18 though 21 until all the leaves are completed.

23 Side-load the short chisel edge of a ⅜-inch (10mm) angle brush with Dusty Mauve. Make a U-stroke at the mouth (or center opening) of the rose.

24 Double-load the short end of the chisel of a ⅜-inch (10mm) angle brush with Dusty Mauve and the long end of the chisel in White (make sure to load this several times to build a lot of paint on your brush). Lay and blend the edge loaded with White facing upward (toward the outside edges of the rose). Stroke an upside-down U-stroke for the back center part of the rose.

25 Move your brush down slightly inside the mouth of the rose and make two or three more smaller upside-down U-strokes to give the appearance of more petals.

26 Continuing with the same brush, pull a comma stroke (in this case, on the left side) for the bottom petal of the rose (keep the White-loaded longer edge toward the outside edge of the petal).

27 Pull a comma on the bottom right of the rose, sliding the overlapping edges of the petals as you ride along on the chisel of the brush to create the tail of the stroke.

28 Pull the next comma on the left side (next to and slightly overlapping the first stroke).

29 Pull the next comma on the right side (next to and slightly overlapping the second stroke).

30 Starting at the outer left edge of the rose center, pull a half U-stroke to the front center (keep the White edge facing up). Stop at the widest point of the stroke.

31 Now pull a half U-stroke starting from the outside right edge. Overlap slightly at the center front of the rose.

32 Pull another comma stroke (one on the right and one on the left) above and around the rose center. Pull additional comma strokes if needed to fill any background spaces.

34 Pull a narrow S-stroke at the base of the rosebud as the top of the stem.

33 Double-load either your no. 8 flat or ⅜-inch (10mm) angle brush, then pull narrow S-strokes at the base of the rosebuds (the rosebuds are painted the same way the first full rose centers are painted).

35 Use a no. 0 script liner to make linework for stems and tendrils.

36 Mix Sachet Pink plus Neutral Gel with a palette knife on your acrylic palette paper.

37 Load your 1-inch (25mm) flat in the mixture from step 36. Lay your brush crossways and paint on the trimwork on all the edges and the dowel on the top (that is used for the handle). Wait about a day for painting to dry completely. Apply several coats of varnish to all surfaces (letting dry between each coat), inside and out.

Completed sewing box.
See page 116 for photo of other side of box.

INDEX